Photo by Tom Soper

LISA THOMPSON

worked as a Radio Broadcast Assistant first at the BBC and then for an independent production company making plays and comedy programmes. She grew up in Essex and now lives in Suffolk with her family.

THE GOLDFISH BOY was one of the bestselling debuts of 2017 and was shortlisted for a number of prizes, including the Waterstones Children's Book Prize. Her stunning second book, THE LIGHT JAR, was chosen as the Children's Book of the Week in the *Times*, the *Guardian* and the *Observer* on publication, THE DAY I WAS ERASED was Children's Book of the Week in the *Times* and THE ROLLERCOASTER BOY was Children's Book of the Week in the *Sunday Times*.

Other books by Lisa Thompson

The Goldfish Boy
The Light Jar
The Day I Was Erased
The Boy Who Fooled the World
The Graveyard Riddle
The Rollercoaster Boy

THE TREASURE HUNTERS

LISA THOMPSON

SCHOLASTIC

Published in the UK by Scholastic, 2023
1 London Bridge, London, SE1 9BG
Scholastic Ireland, 89E Lagan Road, Dublin Industrial Estate,
Glasnevin, Dublin, D11 HP5F

SCHOLASTIC and associated logos are trademarks and/or
registered trademarks of Scholastic Inc.

Text © Lisa Thompson, 2023
Illustrations © Gemma Correll, 2023

The right of Lisa Thompson and Gemma Correll to be identified
as the author and illustrator of this work has been asserted by them under the
Copyright, Designs and Patents Act 1988.

ISBN 978 0702 30160 5

A CIP catalogue record for this book is available from the British Library.

Printed and bound in Great Britain in Clays Ltd, Elcograf S.p.A
Paper made from wood grown in sustainable forests and
other controlled sources.

FSC
www.fsc.org

MIX
Paper | Supporting
responsible forestry
FSC® C018072

3 5 7 9 10 8 6 4 2

This is a work of fiction. Names, characters, places, incidents
and dialogues are products of the author's imagination or are used
fictitiously. Any resemblance to actual people, living or dead,
events or locales is entirely coincidental.

www.scholastic.co.uk

For Claire, Emma, Kelly and Natalie

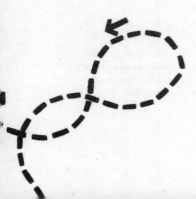

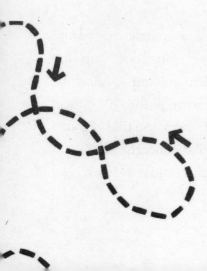

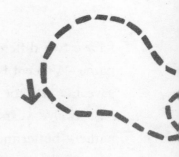

Chapter One

A Zombie Couldn't Solve a Rubik's Cube

Lots of people think that if you play video games too much you'll turn into a zombie. That's rubbish. Did you know there is real science that proves that gaming can actually make you smarter? Playing computer games can improve your coordination, decision-making and problem-solving skills. A zombie wouldn't be able to solve a Rubik's cube, would it? But a gamer probably could. So that is your evidence right there, as far as I'm concerned.

I guess you could say that, because of gaming,

1

I have two different names. First, there is my real name – Vincent Forbes. That's the name my parents gave me and the one I've been known by for the past twelve years. But then there is my gaming name – butterfingers55. And, no, my fingers don't resemble lumps of butter. I chose that name because of something my mum said when I was little. She and Dad had noticed that I was quite late at crawling and walking, and then as I got older I was always dropping stuff and seemed extra clumsy. My older brother, Ewan, wasn't like that in the slightest so I guess that made it even more noticeable. Whenever I dropped something, Mum would say, "Oops, butter fingers!" as if I had buttery, slippery hands and that was why I was always having to pick things up from the floor.

Things got a bit more interesting when my teacher in primary school made a comment on my end-of-term report.

She wrote: *Vincent's writing resembles a spider that has walked through ink before performing a waltz around the paper. He is always forgetting to bring things to school, loses his pencils and is generally very, very disorganized.*

Mum complained to the school about that, but I

thought it was a fair comment. My handwriting *was* shocking. I told Mum that I knew what I wanted to write, but my fingers wouldn't control the pen to make the letters come out properly. And I did struggle to remember stuff and be organized like everyone else. After an apology from my teacher, a few tests and lots of questions, it was decided that I had mild dyspraxia, also known as Developmental Coordination Disorder or DCD. It's not a big deal. I mean, I'll probably never be able to juggle, and I really, really do not like sports one little bit. It takes me a lot of effort to manage things other people find easy, like packing my school bag or remembering stuff, but I'm AMAZING at computer games. Well, one, at least.

I got my console on my birthday last year. Mum, Dad and Ewan sat on the sofa and watched me pull the wrapping paper from a big white box.

"Oh, wow!" I said when I saw what it was. "I didn't know I was getting one of these!"

"Your mum read an article about how it might help with your fine motor skills," said Dad. When I was little I thought that my 'fine motor skills' were something to do with driving a car, but in fact it means learning how to control the smaller muscles in my hands. The ones that help you to hold a pen and use scissors.

"So, Vincent? What do you think?" asked Mum. I was almost speechless, partly because I knew how much games consoles cost but also because I was surprised that they felt I needed help. Did they think I was that bad?

"It's amazing!" I said. I grinned at the three of them but inside I felt a bit panicky. What if I couldn't do it, like all the other things I couldn't quite manage, like riding a bike or hitting a ball with a bat? There was a very big chance that they'd just wasted a lot of money.

Ewan got off the sofa.

"I'll set it up for you in my old room, if you like? There's more space in there," he said, brushing his fluffy ginger hair out of his eyes. Ewan had moved in with Dad not long before my birthday because Dad lived closer to Ewan's college. When Ewan lived with me and Mum, he had to get two different buses, and if he missed one, Mum would have to do a long drive to pick him up. It was weird not having my big brother around. The house felt empty and I missed not seeing him every day.

It didn't take long for Ewan to get all the fiddly leads into the back of the console and get it working.

Mum said she didn't want me to play online for now but I had two games to try: a football one that came free with the console and a driving game that Dad had bought for me. Ewan put the football game in first and I grabbed the controller and got ready. Ewan showed me where to click – he seemed to know exactly what to do – but when the game started I could only make my player go round in circles. I threw the controller down on the floor.

"Don't be like that," said Ewan. "I'm sure the driving game will be easier."

But it wasn't. I couldn't control the car at all and I just kept crashing into the barrier. Ewan said it was because I needed to practise and that I couldn't expect to play brilliantly straight away. Although that didn't stop him having a go and winning three races one after the other. But then my brother was like that. He was good at *everything*.

When I realized I wasn't any good I quickly lost interest in gaming. Occasionally Mum and Dad asked if I was enjoying playing on the console and I lied, saying it was great. But in reality it wasn't long before it sat untouched in Ewan's room, covered in a thin layer of dust. A couple of months later, however, I saw an advert on TV which changed everything.

The advert came on during the commercial break for a reality singing competition that Mum and I watched every Saturday evening. She got up to put the kettle on, and I kicked my legs up on to the sofa and sprawled out. A deep, thunderous sound caught my attention and I stared at the TV. On the screen was a CGI image of a man standing by the ocean and watching a galleon-style ship crashing into the waves. He was tall with dark skin and was wearing a long, grey coat that rippled in the breeze. The bottom half of his face was hidden behind a pale yellow scarf. A deep voice boomed over the graphics:

> *"Fabian has made mistakes.*
> *He's walked alone.*
> *Across continents and along coastlines.*
> *Searching.*
> *Looking.*
> *Hoping."*

The screen focused on Fabian's haunted eyes as they stared out. He had a deep scar across one of his eyebrows, and he looked like a man who had seen things that no one else could even imagine.

"Now he has the chance
To make amends,
To put things right.
To return what was lost."

The graphics changed and Fabian was fighting a goblin-like creature. Now he was rolling on the ground wrestling with a giant black cat. The footage changed again to a close-up of a sword which had five empty holes in its handle, and then Fabian was jumping across the rooftops of a medieval-looking village. The advert slowed down and Fabian stood before a frail old woman who was behind the counter of an old apothecary shop. The shelves around her were crammed with bottles of different-coloured liquids. It then cut to the final shot: Fabian standing on the peak of a snow-capped mountain, his coat still flapping in the breeze and his eyes looking tortured as if he was carrying a great weight on his shoulders. Then the voiceover asked a question that made my stomach fizzle with excitement.

"Are you brave enough to enter the world of ...
'BATTLE DOOM?'"

I felt my heart pounding and I almost shouted back at the TV: "I AM! I'M BRAVE ENOUGH!" It looked utterly incredible. I *had* to have this game.

I had some money in my bank account that I'd saved from Christmas and my birthday, so the next day I asked Mum if she could order it for me. A couple of days later, when I got home from school, there was a brown jiffy bag with my game inside sitting on the kitchen counter. Mum said I had to do my homework and eat dinner before I played it. After dinner I wiped down the table and the kitchen counters (I'd dropped so many plates and mugs in the past that Mum said I didn't need to help load the dishwasher) As soon as I'd finished helping clear up, I grabbed the envelope and ran up to Ewan's old room. It still smelled of his deodorant spray, which wasn't surprising because he used to put so much on that it was probably embedded in the walls.

I sat on his squeaky, twirly chair by the console and ripped open the jiffy bag. I took out the box and held the game in my hand. Fabian was on the front and, even though the pale yellow scarf hid half of his face, I could still tell by his haunted eyes that he was pained and troubled. I leaned to one side and looked into Ewan's mirror on the wall. Did my eyes look pained and troubled like Fabian's? I thought they probably did.

I switched the console on, and my fingers tingled as I put the disc into the machine. It whirred and buzzed for a few minutes while the game loaded, and then it began with an introduction to Fabian's story.

The story was pretty hard to understand, to be honest, but I got the gist of it: Fabian had been an important person in his town, like a mayor or something, but he was banished for doing something wrong. (I'm not sure what it was he actually did that upset everyone but I don't think it mattered.) He was really sad about not being allowed home so he decided that he was going to make it up to his fellow townspeople by finding the five missing stones of the Scorpion Sword. The sword was really important to them for some reason or another – I think they skimmed over that bit just so that the player can get to the end of the game to find out what the sword is actually for. Fabian has to travel the five regions of this fantasy world to retrieve each stone for the sword. Then and only then he would be accepted back home.

The screen moved on to the actual game and I found myself staring at Fabian's back. I pushed my joystick left and right and he turned in each direction.

Then he just stood there, the movement of his back telling me that he was breathing as he waited for me to decide where we were going to start on our adventure together.

It was easy to control Fabian and make him walk around and do things, and even when there were difficult parts, like climbing up things, I didn't get frustrated like I had with the other games. I was already too absorbed in the story. When I looked at the clock, it was hours past my bedtime. I saved the game and switched the console off, then ran downstairs. Mum had fallen asleep on the sofa in front of the TV.

"Mum? It's bedtime," I said, gently shaking her arm.

"Oh, Vincent. I must have dropped off for a bit," she said, her eyelids heavy. Fortunately she didn't notice that I was still dressed or how late it was.

That night when I closed my eyes I saw Fabian running across hillsides and through alleyways, jumping across moats and high rooftops, and I felt a smile spread across my face. I couldn't wait to play *Battle Doom*, after school tomorrow.

At last I had found something that I was good at.

Chapter Two

Out of Your Depth

My dad loves a chat and one of his favourite things to talk about is how to improve yourself. He's a life coach and motivational speaker, and people pay him lots of money to tell them how to be 'the best they can be'. I go with him every week to watch Ewan play football, and it's then that he likes to tell me stuff that I guess he tells his clients.

"You know that feeling when you're in a swimming pool and you can't quite reach the bottom, Vincent?" he said as we stood on the sideline. "That's how life should feel: just a little bit of a challenge."

We clapped as Ewan scored the fifth goal of the game.

"It sounds scary," I said.

"It's not scary. It's exciting! Living life just out of your depth opens up endless possibilities," said Dad. I kept quiet. I had a feeling his comment was leading somewhere. They usually did.

"The singer David Bowie said that," Dad continued. "Live life just out of your depth. It keeps things fresh and exciting."

I thought back to my swimming lessons when I was six years old. At the start of each lesson we all had to line up along the side and hold on to the rail. I was one of the tallest so the teacher told me to go nearer the deep end, even though I couldn't swim properly yet. Everyone else had their feet flat on the floor, but I had my big toes stretched as far as they could and even then they were barely brushing the bottom of the pool. I was almost out of my depth but it hadn't felt exciting. I was just trying desperately not to snort water up my nose. I wondered if David Bowie had ever felt his toes scrape the bottom of a swimming pool. I seriously doubted it. Besides, I wasn't really interested in having adventures, and I was quite happy having my feet firmly on the ground, thank you very much.

We watched Ewan tackle someone to win back the ball and hurtle towards the goal again.

"Go on, Ewan! That's it!" cried Dad. There was another ripple of applause as he scored again. Ewan waved at us as his teammates patted him on the back.

"Maybe you could take up a hobby like your brother?" said Dad. "I was thinking you could try tennis, perhaps?"

And there it was. Dad's weekly attempt at getting me to try to be 'more like Ewan'.

"Maybe," I said. Even though there was no way I'd be any good at tennis. I'm sure he knew that I was lying but Dad grinned all the same.

A few minutes later the referee blew his whistle for the end of the match and we began a slow walk towards the burger van to get our bacon rolls.

"How's school going, Vincent?" he said.

I paused for a second. He never usually asked about school so I was a bit surprised.

"It's fine," I said.

Dad nodded. "And you've got some nice friends, yes? Your mum and I haven't met any of them yet. You can always ask them over, you know."

I stared down at the grass. "Yeah, I know. Everyone is a bit busy, I guess."

Dad was about to ask me something else when Ewan ran over, his face bright red, snot smeared across his cheek. He looked really happy.

"Did you see my last goal, Dad? It went between the keeper's legs!"

"We were all watching, you know?" I mumbled. Dad took Ewan's football bag.

"You were amazing! How many goals is that this season now?" said Dad.

Ewan shrugged.

"I don't know. I'll have to ask," he said. The fact my brother didn't know how many goals he'd scored didn't mean he was cocky. It was more that it wasn't a big deal to him so he just hadn't kept track. He found all sports easy. And college. And making friends. And exams. In fact, Ewan found *life* easy.

We got to the burger van queue and Dad turned to me.

"You go and grab a seat, Vincent," said Dad. "Ketchup?"

"Yes, please," I said, heading to our usual bench.

When I sat down I thought about telling Dad about *Battle Doom* and how many missions I'd solved. I had almost reached the final level even though it was one of the hardest video games out there. It had taken me five weeks of missions and now I had just one more jewel to find: a diamond. Once I'd placed that diamond into its rightful position in the Scorpion Sword, I would have completed the entire game, and Fabian could return to his town, Riverlock, triumphant. The more I thought about it, the more I thought I *should* tell Dad. I wasn't scoring goals or anything, but he'd still be proud, wouldn't he? I looked up. Dad and Ewan were still in the queue, but they seemed to be recreating one of Ewan's tackles and were laughing. Dad threw his arm around Ewan's neck and ruffled his hair.

I turned back round. Maybe telling Dad about *Battle Doom* wasn't such a good idea. He wouldn't get it.

While I waited, a boy and a woman headed towards me and I realized I knew him. His name was Jonny and we were in the same English class. As they got closer, I straightened up and smiled, but he completely blanked me and just walked past. I don't think he recognized me at all.

Although, I doubt many of the pupils in my year at Linley High would recognize me on the street. You see, the thing is, I'm kind of invisible in secondary school. Back in primary, things were a lot easier. Yes, I'd felt awkward because of having extra help with my writing and I got moaned at for not being organized enough, but mostly it had been fine and I had friends. But then we'd all headed to different schools and suddenly I was alone. The first term went by and then another and, before I knew it, I'd been there nine months and everyone had paired up apart from me. Going to school felt like a mission.

When I got into *Battle Doom* I decided to approach the school day like I was Fabian and it was just another quest to solve. I began to run a daily gauntlet of ways to look like I wasn't actually on my own *all* of the time. I made sure that I was first in the classroom so I could position myself in a corner seat and not seem bothered when everyone else sat with their mates. At break and lunchtimes my aim was to appear really busy to everyone else. Sometimes I went to the library and pretended to browse the shelves, then I might head to the school noticeboard and act like there was something I was trying to find; then I'd go to the toilet, and then I'd walk the playground and around the outside of the school building in a purposeful manner. The final challenge was to be out of the school gates before everyone else gathered in groups to walk together. If anyone noticed me hurrying then they'd just think that I had somewhere important to be.

Which was true in a lot of ways. I had to get home quickly so that I could finish my homework and then I'd have more time to play *Battle Doom*. After all, Fabian was depending on me.

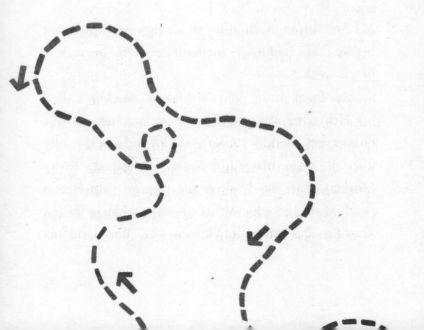

Chapter Three

The Worst Form Time. Ever

My first lesson on Monday morning was French, but before that I had to get through the worst form time of the week.

My form tutor was a history teacher called Mr Hearn; he was one of the popular ones. He was always very friendly and smiled a lot and he especially liked it when his students were 'engaged'. Every Monday, after he'd taken the register, Mr Hearn perched on the edge of his desk for what he called 'chat time'. It was a simple idea – he chose students at random and asked them to tell the class what they did at the weekend. Considering no one said much beyond a few words, I was surprised he hadn't given up with the whole thing but he hadn't abandoned the idea yet.

"OK, 7A!" he said as he rolled the sleeves of his shirt up to his elbows. "We have a bit of time before your first lesson so let's hear what exciting things you've been getting up to in the last two days, shall we? Josh? Shall we begin with you?" I thought that Mr Hearn was being a bit optimistic here. Josh Park was the least engaged student in the whole year.

"So, what did you get up to this weekend, Josh?" said Mr Hearn, tilting his head to one side.

Josh was slumped forward with his chin resting on his desk. He was rolling a pencil back and forth with his hand.

"Just stuff," said Josh, not looking up.

"That's great!" said Mr Hearn, not even slightly discouraged. "And what sort of stuff was that? Would you like to tell us?"

Josh stopped rolling the pencil for a second and then he shrugged his shoulders.

"No, not really," he said.

Mr Hearn nodded and stood up. "That's absolutely

fine as well," he said. "You don't have to share but remember I really would like it if you did. I'd like you to all be *engaged*."

He walked around the classroom and appeared to be thinking of who to choose next. My heart pounded, hoping he wouldn't pick me.

"How about you, Lena? What did you do this weekend?" said Mr Hearn, leaning on a bookcase.

Lena was quiet for a moment and then she began to speak. "I did some research," she said, so quietly it was almost inaudible.

Mr Hearn's eyes lit up. "That's wonderful! What are you researching? Is it for a school project?"

Lena quickly shook her head. "No. I was looking at my grandpa's work. He was an investigator before he died."

Mr Hearn nodded his head, waiting for her to say more.

Scarlett, Melanie and Holly, who sat behind Lena, began to giggle and whisper to each other behind their hands.

"He sounds like an interesting man. Can you tell us a little bit about what he investigated?" said Mr Hearn.

Lena twisted round in her seat so that she was

facing more of the class. She seemed to have perked up and she was smiling. She spoke a little louder this time.

"My grandpa was a *really* clever man and he knew about all these amazing things that happen around the world that other people don't really know about." As she spoke, she waved her hands, getting quite animated. "He investigated things like sightings of ghosts or maybe people who have vanished into thin air, *and* he once went to Norway to look for vampires!"

There were a few seconds of silence and then the whole class erupted into laughter. Lena's smile vanished.

"What *are* you talking about?" said Scarlett. "Vampires?! Was your grandpa senile or something?" Lena's face dropped and she turned back in her seat. "You are *such* a weirdo, Kaminski."

What Lena had said was a bit ... out there. And there was no way Scarlett was going to let her get away with that.

Everyone was still laughing as Mr Hearn went back to the front of the class.

"That's enough," he said. "Quieten down, everybody." He didn't spot Scarlett kick the back of

Lena's chair, making her jolt forward.

After a bit, everyone stopped laughing and Mr Hearn began again.

"Right. Let's move on, shall we? How about you, Vincent?" said Mr Hearn. "What exciting things did you get up to this weekend?"

My stomach flipped.

"I … erm … I went to watch my brother play football," I said.

"Oh, wow. That sounds great fun! Do you play as well?" asked Mr Hearn.

I shook my head.

"OK," he said. "So did you do anything else?"

I thought about how I'd spent the rest of the weekend playing *Battle Doom*, much to Mum's dismay. The whole gaming thing had been her idea in the first place but now she didn't like me being on it for too long. I had taken Fabian to an abandoned castle on the outskirts of the village of Brunfawn. I'd thought the diamond could be in there but so far I'd found nothing apart from a really annoying travelling hawker who kept following me, trying to get me to spend my coins.

"Vincent?" said Mr Hearn. "Was there anything else you did at the weekend?"

"Just a bit of gaming," I muttered.

Mr Hearn smiled and nodded as if that was the most fascinating thing he'd ever heard in his whole life.

"That's great. Thank you for sharing," he said.

I suddenly remembered that during the game the alarm I'd set on my phone went off. It was set every evening to remind me to pack my school bag ready for the next day. I had been so absorbed in *Battle Doom* that I'd switched the alarm off and forgotten all about it. It was highly unlikely I'd have my French book with me for the next lesson. My teachers knew I had dyspraxia, but some were more sympathetic than others. My French teacher, Ms Davis, was one of those who got frustrated and couldn't understand why my work was sometimes in a muddle, why my homework sheets were completed but still lying on my bedroom floor.

Mr Hearn went round a few more students, who admitted to trampolining going to the cinema and having a haircut, and then he returned to the front of the class.

"Thank you, 7A. It's been really lovely to hear about how you spent your weekends," he said. "Now tomorrow in assembly Ms Bell is going to make a very special announcement. It's about an amazing opportunity for some lucky pupils, and I hope you'll listen very carefully."

As soon as the bell rang signalling our first lesson, I jumped out of my seat and immediately smashed my leg into the desk. Having dyspraxia means that I'm always bumping into things, which was another reason to get out of class before the big rush. I managed to scoot around all the other students who were still bending down to pick up their bags and hurried out of the classroom. The corridor was still quiet and I trotted as quickly as I could across the school foyer. I thought about what to say to Ms Davis about forgetting my books, and I decided I'd tell her as soon as I walked into class. Owning up straight away was the best way to handle it. Yes, she'd be annoyed, probably, but I'd earn a bit of credit for being honest immediately. It was a short walk to the language block, and I headed to my class and to my usual seat at the back.

Mission accomplished.

Everyone piled in and Ms Davis began the lesson. Then I realized it had been mission accomplished *apart* from remembering to tell Ms Davis about my books. I'd blown it.

Fortunately, Ms Davis wasn't too angry when I owned up halfway through the lesson, but my English teacher, Mrs Edwards, was another matter. Hers was the last lesson of the day and I'd left my copy of *Of Mice And Men* at home for the third lesson running. She told me, in front of the whole class, that I'd forget my own head if it wasn't attached to my neck. A few people sniggered at that, but I'd heard it about a million times and still didn't think it was very funny.

She loaned me another copy and then droned on and on about the story, but all I could think about was getting home to *Battle Doom*. Eventually the bell went and I quickly packed my bag but I struggled to get one of my folders in. Everyone else was leaving and the longer it took for me to get out, the more likely I'd get caught up amongst the groups of friends.

"A few of us are going to the high street to get some chips. Do you wanna come?" said Jonny. I froze as I half did the zip up on my bag. Why was Jonny talking to me? Maybe he *had* seen me at football yesterday after all? I could text Mum and tell her I'd be a bit late. She wouldn't mind. I turned to face him.

"Sure!" I said.

Jonny frowned at me. "What?" he said.

"I said sure. About going to get some chips."

Jonny looked awkward. "Um. I was talking to Aaron," he said. I turned to my left just as Aaron swung his rucksack over his shoulder and the two of them walked out of the classroom.

I took my time and repacked my bag. For a change I was the last person to leave the classroom, and when I got out on to the playground the place was deserted apart from a lone seagull pecking at an empty crisp packet.

I began a slow walk home.

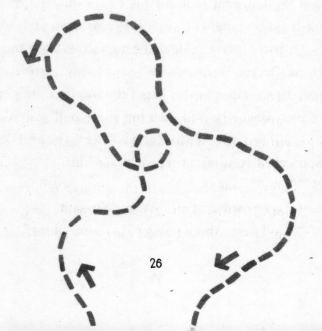

Chapter Four

Assembly

The announcement Mr Hearn had mentioned in form came the next day in an assembly led by our chemistry teacher, Ms Bell. As everyone settled down she walked on to the stage at the front of the hall. Behind her was a big screen.

"Year Seven, I am pleased to say that an amazing opportunity has presented itself to us," said Ms Bell. "We have been asked if we would like to send a group of students to the annual Wilderness Warrior Challenge in just ten days' time!" There were murmurs in the crowd, and I guessed a few students must have already heard of it, but I hadn't. Ms Bell was one of those strange people who loved extreme sports like running over mountains at night-time and stuff. I guessed that's why she was in charge of telling us about any kind of "challenge".

"This is a trip that isn't available to all schools as the costs can be extremely high," continued Ms Bell. "And we have only been given this chance because another school has had to pull out at the last minute due to an administrative error."

The screen behind her lit up.

"So, what is the Wilderness Warrior Challenge all about? Well, let me show you right now."

I sat upright in my chair so I could see a bit better. Assemblies were usually very dull so it was nice to have something to look at for a change. Ms Bell clicked a clicker and the first slide appeared on the screen. It read:

THE WILDERNESS WARRIOR CHALLENGE

DO YOU HAVE WHAT IT TAKES TO SURVIVE THE WILD?

On the slide were pictures of mountains, forests, lakes and streams. Ms Bell turned to us, smiling.

"The Wilderness Warrior Challenge will test your resilience, your commitment, your team-building skills and your endurance." She jabbed her finger towards us as she spoke.

Scarlett Franklin, who was sitting next to me, gave a bored huff. She seemed to be more interested in her nails than listening to Ms Bell and she nibbled on one, studied it for a moment, then moved on to the next. Beside her was Melanie, who was inspecting the ends of her hair. They were usually in a group of three with Holly, but apparently they weren't talking to her right now. The three of them were always falling out.

Ms Bell continued. "Over three days, in the tough terrain of the Hamlin District National Park, you and your team will use your hiking and survival skills to get you across the finish line."

Ms Bell clicked again and the slide changed to a picture of a group of four kids sitting by a tent with their arms around each other. They looked a bit muddy, and I noticed one had some sort of tourniquet around her leg, but they were all grinning and looked very, very happy.

"Before the challenge you will be taught basic

map-reading skills, you'll practise putting up your tent, and learn how to cook on a camp stove. There will be checkpoints throughout the route where you will meet up with the Challengers, who are fully trained Wilderness Warriors staff who will ensure that you are fit and well. You'll also be walking in view of some pretty dramatic scenery – that of the glorious Fortune Mountain. In fact, you'll be camping in the surrounding foothills of the mountain on the first night."

She clicked again and this time there was a photograph of four more grinning children, each with a giant rucksack on their shoulders. In the distance loomed a mountain dusted in snow. It reminded me a little of a mountain in *Battle Doom*.

"There is also a competition on this trip to win a cash prize!" said Ms Bell. A few heads perked up when they heard the word 'cash'. Ms Bell carried on. "If your team is the first to reach the final checkpoint without breaking any of the rules, then each of you will be crowned Ultimate Wilderness Warriors. Your school will then be awarded a substantial sum."

A few students groaned and went back to fidgeting when they realized the winning money wouldn't be going to the actual team members. Just then there was an almighty crash at the back of the hall. Ms Bell peered over our heads to see what had happened. Mr Gibbs, one of the art teachers, was already out of his seat and striding to the back.

"I might have known it would be you, Josh Park. Why do you have to be such a clown, eh? Up you get and out you go," said Mr Gibbs. Everyone turned round to see what was going on. Josh was sprawled on the floor, laughing. I guessed that he had been rocking on the back legs of his chair, which I'd seen him do countless times in lessons. He always got told off for it but it never seemed to stop him.

"I said, UP AND OUT!" shouted Mr Gibbs.

Josh slowly got to his feet. His shirt was hanging out of his trousers and his tie was half-undone. He grinned at everyone then turned and lolloped out of the hall with Mr Gibbs following him.

"As I was saying," said Ms Bell. "This last-minute opportunity is an invitation-only trip, and we have enough places for one team of four. I have already been chatting to your form tutors and we have come up with our chosen students. If you are one of the lucky ones, your grown-up will be receiving an email this evening. There is also some funding available from the school to help towards the cost of any kit you might need to purchase. The first meeting to discuss the trip is being held tomorrow after school as we have such a short time to prepare. The chosen pupils will join me then to find out more."

A few of the sporty kids in front of me began to chat about how much they wanted to do the trip, but I couldn't think of anything worse. This had Ewan's name written all over it; he'd have been begging to go. Luckily, I was pretty sure Ms Bell had no idea I existed so there was no worry that my parents would be getting an email.

"I hope that those of you who are given this opportunity will take it with a sense of adventure in your hearts. It will be a memorable weekend that will most certainly stay with you for many years to come," said Ms Bell. "We hope this will be the first of many trips like this, so if you haven't been chosen this time, there will be other opportunities."

Our head teacher, Mrs Dann, closed the assembly with a few boring announcements about litter and the sports hall toilets, and then it was over.

While we waited for our row to be excused, Scarlett slumped in her chair and let out another of her loud huffs.

"That was *so* boring," she said. "Why would

anyone choose to go on a weekend like that?" I didn't say anything as I assumed that she wasn't really talking to me.

"Did anyone hear where the weekend was?" said a voice behind me. It was Lena.

"What does it matter to you, Kaminski?" said Scarlett. "Urgh. You're so … *strange*."

"Yeah, you must take after your vampire-hunting grandpa," said Melanie. The two of them began to laugh and Lena flushed pink.

It was our turn to leave and I hurried off, but Lena caught me up and tapped my arm.

"Did you hear where the weekend was?" she asked.

"Um, some national park, I think. She mentioned Fortune Mountain so it's wherever that is."

Lena's face broke into a grin. "I knew it," she said. "Thanks, Vincent."

She rushed off and as she headed down the corridor I realized that she was the first student in nine months who had actually called me by my name.

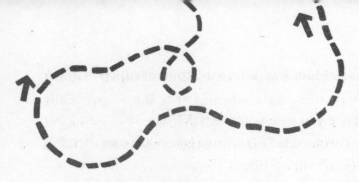

Chapter Five

Not Waving but Drowning

When I got home from school Mum was sitting at her small desk in the corner of our lounge. She used this area as an office as she worked from home running a small marketing company. Like Dad, she loved her job and she worked long hours.

"Hi, Vincent," said Mum, not turning around. "How was school?"

"Fine," I said. There was no need to tell her about forgetting my books. It wasn't like I'd got into trouble or anything.

But Mum had a frowny, concerned look on her face.

"Are you sure school is OK?" she said, tilting her head to one side. "Everything good with your friends?"

"Yes," I lied. "Why?"

Mum had no idea that I didn't have any friends and I wanted to keep it that way. I was absolutely fine with it, but I knew she'd worry about me, thinking I was lonely or something silly like that.

"I'm just checking on you. Your dad is ringing you later. He's got something he wants to talk to you about," she said, smiling now.

I frowned, wondering what it could be. He was probably going to ask me if I wanted to go rock climbing or something. There was always another thing for me to try so I could be a bit more like Ewan. I huffed to myself but Mum was looking back at her laptop and hadn't noticed.

"Remember to do your homework before you go on that game," said Mum. "I don't like you spending so much time on it, Vincent."

"But *you* bought it for me, Mum, remember?" I said.

Fortunately her mobile rang so I was spared another lecture.

I went to the kitchen and grabbed a bag of crisps. The house was much quieter now Ewan didn't live here any more, but at least there was more food to eat.

I went up to my room and began my history homework, which I didn't actually mind because we were learning about the Middle Ages and some of the stuff we were covering, like castles and villages, was a bit like *Battle Doom*. I was itching to get back to my game. The Scorpion Sword was looking pretty magnificent now that it contained the ruby, emerald, sapphire and amethyst. Once I had the diamond I could slot it into the final hole, and Fabian would return to his hometown of Riverlock a hero.

I was just answering a question about where the best place to build a castle would be (the top of a hill, obviously) when my mobile rang.

"Hi, Vincent! Can you hear me?" shouted Dad over the roar of traffic. I remembered that he had been giving a talk to some businesses in London that day.

"Hi, Dad!" I said. "How did your speech go?"

"Really well! In fact, I'm pretty sure a few lives will have been changed." He chuckled. Dad had a way of sounding like he was showing off, but he was actually really proud of what he did, and he wasn't embarrassed about it like some people would be.

"That's great, Dad!" I said.

Dad said something to someone in the background. I recognized their voice immediately.

"Is that Ewan?" I said. "What's he doing there?"

There was the rumbling sound of a bus going past, and then Dad began to shout again so I held the phone away from my ear a little bit.

"Your brother didn't have to go into college today, and he said he wanted to come and see me in action," said Dad.

I felt a stab of jealousy right in the centre of my ribs. Dad and Ewan said something between them that I couldn't hear and they both laughed.

"What was that?" I said. "I can't hear you."

"Oh, it was nothing," said Dad. "Ewan just said something funny, that's all."

I wished that Ewan wasn't there so I could talk to Dad on my own for a change. I knew he didn't mean anything by it, but it felt like he was always in the background chipping in on our conversation. When Dad first moved out, he told us he felt like he had too much space around him without us being there. He made sure to make time for both of us, but now it felt like Ewan was filling in all the gaps.

"Are you still there, Vincent?" said Dad.

"Yes. I'm here."

"So I was ringing because I got an email today from your school about an *amazing* opportunity," said Dad.

I wondered what he was talking about for a moment and then I remembered Ms Bell's assembly that morning and the slides showing the kids on the camping trip. I suddenly felt sick.

"Um. What's that?" I croaked.

"The school have invited you to take part in the Wilderness Warrior Challenge! Can you believe it?" said Dad. He sounded so excited. "This is big news, son. I know all about these challenges from work. It'll be amazing for you!"

My mind began to race, trying to find the right words to immediately get out of it. There was absolutely no way I was going on this trip.

"I don't want to," I said. I heard a police siren in the background. It got louder and louder then began to fade away.

"What did you say, Vincent? I can't hear you," yelled Dad.

"I said I DON'T WANT TO DO IT," I shouted. "I CAN'T do it!"

Dad laughed. "Of course you want to do it! And the school wouldn't have asked you if they didn't think it was something you could do, would they?"

I could feel a sense of panic beginning to engulf my chest.

"They can ask someone else," I said.

There was a fumbling sound. Dad must have passed the phone to Ewan as the next thing it was his voice booming into my eardrum.

"Vincent, you'd be crazy to miss this!" said my brother. "I've *always* wanted to go on one of these challenges and I never got the chance. You'll absolutely love it!"

There was another fumble and Dad came back on the line.

"Did you hear that? Your brother would love to do this! You can use some of his kit – it's high-quality gear. Isn't that right, Ewan?"

They said something between them again.

"Dad? Dad!" I yelled. "I'm not doing it!" I didn't want to argue with him, but why couldn't he see that I wasn't like him or Ewan? I was happy with how things were. Being at home with Mum and playing *Battle Doom*.

"You've got to start stepping out of your comfort zone a bit, Vincent," said Dad. "It's not good to always feel safe. You don't develop as a person if you stay in your lane all the time."

"But I like it in my lane," I said quietly. I don't think Dad heard me, and then Ewan started saying something about some old walking boots he had that were my size.

"Hey, listen. I've got to go as we're going down to the underground now and I'll lose the signal, but remember you're a winner, Vincent. OK? What are you?"

I opened my mouth to reply but there was a beep as Dad got cut off.

"I'm a winner," I said to my empty bedroom.

I slumped on to my bed, and as I lay there I heard Mum coming up the stairs. She knocked on my door and came in.

"Hi, Vincent," she said. "Is everything OK?"

I frowned at her.

"Did you talk to Dad about me going on that weekend?" I said.

"Yes, love. We talked about it earlier."

I was so angry with her for being in on it as well. "I'm *not* doing it, Mum. And I don't see why the school have asked me to go in the first place! There must be loads of kids who actually *want* to go."

Mum sat down on the end of my bed.

"The thing is, Vincent, the school have noticed that you've been struggling a bit to … fit in," she said.

I gasped.

"What?!" I said. "That's rubbish. I'm fitting in just fine!"

Mum took a long breath.

"Your form tutor has raised some concerns that you might be finding it hard to make friends. He said that whenever he sees you around school you are always on your own."

That explained why Mum was being weird when I got in and asked about my friends! What did Mr Hearn think he was doing saying something like that? Had he been spying on me? He'd called me over to have a chat after registration a couple of weeks ago and asked how I was finding Year Seven. But at the time I thought that he was checking in with everyone and it was just my turn. And, anyway, I'd said that I was fine and he seemed to be OK with that.

"Your father and I have been concerned too. You haven't seen anyone outside of school since you've been there, have you, sweetheart?" said Mum. "Is it true what Mr Hearn said? Has it been a bit of a struggle to make friends?"

I bit my bottom lip and shrugged. Mum sighed.

"I think this weekend would be something amazing for you. It's a chance for you to get out in the fresh air for a bit," she said. "You spend so much time on that game, it'll be a nice change to have some time in the countryside."

"But I hate the outdoors," I said. "I've never been camping; I can't put up a tent and I … I'm just not like Ewan!"

I flopped back on to my pillow and put one arm over my face.

"No, you're not like Ewan," said Mum. "But you have your own talents and skills that you'll bring to the group. There's a chat after school tomorrow where you'll get to meet the rest of your team."

I felt like my side of the argument was becoming weaker and weaker by the second, and I was scrambling to think of what I could say next.

"Come on, Vincent," said Mum. "What's the worst that could happen?"

"I could get bitten by a snake and die," I said. "I could get lost on the hills and get hypothermia or fall down a cliff and break my neck…"

"*Or*," interrupted Mum, "you could actually enjoy it and make some new friends along the way.

Friends that you'll have had some amazing shared experiences with. How about that?"

"But I'm getting to the end of *Battle Doom*, Mum! I need my weekends to complete it." I knew that using a computer game as a reason not to go wasn't going to help me, but it was true. After all, *that* was how I liked to spend my spare time. Not trekking around muddy fields with a bunch of strangers who'd probably hate me.

"Don't be ridiculous, Vincent," said Mum. "You're not missing out on this for a silly computer game."

Inside I wanted to tell her how wrong she was. It was definitely not just a computer game. Solving Fabian's quest was *everything* to me right now. But I knew trying to explain that to my mum was pointless.

"The game will still be here waiting for you when you get back," said Mum.

I felt like my heart was being crushed. "So, that's it? I don't even have a choice?"

Mum looked like she had tears in her eyes, and I wondered if maybe she was finding this whole thing just as hard as I was. But even if she was I didn't care. I couldn't believe she was making me do this.

"Your father and I both agree that you'll make a terrific Wilderness Warrior and that once you take part in this challenge you'll realize it for yourself. We wouldn't be asking you to do it if we didn't think it was the best thing for you."

I rolled over and pulled my pillow over my head. Mum sat there for a few seconds and then she got up and I heard my bedroom door softly close.

My stomach churned. They couldn't exactly drag me there, could they? I needed to be firmer and refuse to go. But then Mr Hearn's comment about me 'struggling' kept playing on my mind. Had he really spotted that I was always on my own? I thought my daily routine was watertight – just keep moving and then no one would be able to tell. But it sounded like it wasn't working after all. Even Mum and Dad had noticed. I took the pillow off my head and clutched it to my stomach.

I thought about Dad's favourite quote about 'living life so that you feel just out of your depth'.

Well, if this was how that felt, then I was pretty sure that I was drowning.

Chapter Six

Mr Hearn the Troublemaker

The next morning when I woke up I had a few blissful seconds where I'd completely forgotten about what had happened the night before. I was still in that warm, fuzzy moment of being half-asleep. The first thing to pop into my brain was *Battle Doom*. There was an old well in the region of Brunfawn, and I'd walked Fabian past it a few times now, thinking it was insignificant, but maybe that was the whole point? Maybe it was supposed to look uninteresting so I didn't check there? I decided that I'd look after school, and then the pit of my stomach lurched and I remembered – there was a meeting after school for the Wilderness Warriors Challenge.

I got up, hoping that Mum might have rung Dad and told him how obvious it was that I didn't want to go. Maybe they'd come to a decision that forcing me to go was unfair. They might even have emailed the school to say a firm thank-you-but-Vincent-is-just-fine-and-won't-be-going-on-the-trip message. But at breakfast Mum seemed even more adamant.

"You shouldn't not do things because you're scared, Vincent," said Mum. "There are always things in life that scare us, and you just have to face up to them."

"I'm not *scared*. It's a ridiculous weekend and I don't want to do it!" I said. "I can't believe that you are making me, Mum. How could you?"

I could see Mum wavering a little and I felt a glimmer of hope. She and I were more alike than me and Dad. She liked being at home and pottering around, just like I did. It was Dad and Ewan who were the outdoorsy ones, who set themselves challenges all the time. But just when I thought I was actually getting through to her, she shook her head and any doubts she had must have disappeared.

"No, Vincent. This will be good for you. We know it as your parents, and Mr Hearn knows it as your teacher."

I wanted to scream at her. It was so unfair that everyone was making these decisions without my input. Mum tied her long red hair into a bun on top of her head and put two slices of bread into the toaster, slamming the button down firmly. I turned and ran upstairs. I definitely would *not* be eating breakfast with her today.

When I went into form time, I expected Mr Hearn to say something to me but he was busy talking to Lena. I walked past Josh, who was swinging on his chair again, and sat in my seat in the corner. I'd packed my school bag last night so at least I had everything I needed today.

Holly and Melanie were sitting in front of me, clearly friends again. Scarlett seemed to be the one out of the group now and she was sitting on her own on the opposite side of the classroom.

"I wonder what saddos have been chosen to go on that wilderness weekend thing," said Holly. "It's probably the usual nerds."

"I think if my parents made me go then I'd ask to be adopted or something," said Melanie. Holly laughed.

"Your parents are lovely!" she said. "I'd rather have your mum than Scarlett's. Have you met her?"

"No!" said Melanie. "What is she like?"

"Well, she's really glamorous and that, but she is *well* mean. I went over there once and she started shouting at Scarlett because she hadn't put her cereal bowl in the dishwasher. I know we all get told off, but this was on another level. Scarlett just stood there and took it and didn't say a *thing*."

"Really?" said Melanie. "That's so weird."

"Yeah," said Holly. "Honestly, her mum is evil."

I glanced over at Scarlett, who looked bored as she gazed around the classroom. Her eyes passed over Melanie and Holly and she scowled as if she knew they were talking about her.

After the register, Mr Hearn told us about a new book club that was starting up in the school library, and then the bell went for our first lesson. I thought I'd got away without him talking to me, but he called me over before I had a chance to escape. He waited for the last student to leave while I hovered by his desk.

"I understand that you'll be taking part in the Wilderness Warriors Challenge, Vincent," he said. "I just wanted to say that I think that is absolutely brilliant."

I shrugged. I had such a large lump in my throat I was worried that if I spoke I'd start getting upset. And I didn't want to cry in front of a teacher. I was also feeling quite angry. If it wasn't for Mr Hearn saying things about me looking lonely then I wouldn't be in this mess. I stared at the floor.

"Do you know what, Vincent? I found school really hard when I was your age," he said. I looked up at him. Mr Hearn was one of the most popular teachers in the school. I couldn't imagine that he'd ever found *anything* hard.

"Why?" I said.

Mr Hearn raised his eyes to the ceiling and screwed up his nose.

"Hmmm. I am telling you this in the strictest of confidence but … I was always getting into trouble. I was in detention most weeks; the head would write letters home to my parents; I was suspended about three times and, well, I think I just lost my way a bit."

I found all of this very hard to believe. "Really?" I said. He nodded.

"There was this one time where I locked the caretaker in the sports hall and threw the key down the drain. I got in *so* much trouble for that one that the school talked to my parents about expelling me.

49

That was the turning point. I had to change or I'd end up ruining my life. It was pretty bad."

"So what happened?" I asked. "Did you get expelled?"

Mr Hearn took a deep breath and intertwined his fingers together around his knee.

"The school spoke to my parents and they decided to send me on a weekend away. It was with other kids who were having issues with behaviour at school. I *really* didn't want to go, I tell you. I shouted and screamed. I was livid about it. But it ended up being the best thing I'd ever done. I made friends on that trip that I still have today. It changed my life. And I think you'll find the Wilderness Warriors will help you too."

I was puzzled. "But I don't get in trouble at school," I said. And it was true. Yes, I was disorganized and forgot my stuff a lot, but I wasn't one of the kids who was always in detention.

"I know you don't. And I know you have extra hurdles to overcome too with your dyspraxia. The other kids don't realize that, do they?"

I shook my head.

"And I know you're very smart, even if you find some of the work a challenge sometimes," said Mr

Hearn with a smile. He was right about that. Any lessons that involved writing essays were the worst as what I wanted to say usually jumbled up in my head. "Sometimes a student might need a little help to find their feet," continued Mr Hearn. "It was when I was on the weekend away that I realized what was at the root of my anger and misbehaviour. Things were quite tough for me at home, but on top of that I didn't have any friends. And to deal with that I was acting up and showing off and doing everything I possibly could to show everyone else that I wasn't bothered. When, in fact, I really was."

I couldn't picture Mr Hearn getting into detention, but then why would he make up something like that?

"Was it the Wilderness Warriors Challenge that you went on?" I asked.

He shook his head. "No. The trip I went on was specifically for kids who were struggling like I was, and who were in trouble at school. The Wilderness Warriors is open to anyone. And I am convinced that you'll enjoy it, Vincent. And if you don't, what's the worst that could happen?"

I was going to tell him about getting bitten by a snake or falling off a mountain or hypothermia, but Mr Hearn picked up his bag and stood up.

"I've got to get to my next class now," he said. "I honestly think you can do this, Vincent. And I think you'll find it will really help you. Go to the meeting after school tonight and find out a bit more."

I didn't quite say, "Yes, OK," but I nodded at him. He smiled back.

"That's great," he said. "And, remember, no telling anyone that I was known as Horror Hearn when I was thirteen. Is that a deal?"

"OK. Deal," I said.

I walked out of the classroom and then I realized that I would be the last person to go into my maths class. Everyone would stare and wonder where I had been and I'd have to sit next to someone who probably wouldn't want me there. I took a deep breath, put my head down and carried on along the corridor.

Chapter Seven

The Team Meeting

When the end-of-school bell went my stomach twisted into a knot. It was time for the Wilderness Warriors Challenge meeting. I made my way to the main hall and went in through the wide doors. Ms Bell was putting some chairs out at the front and she hadn't noticed me. It would have been quite easy for me to just turn around and go home. Sure, everyone would be disappointed in me, but they'd get over it. But then Ms Bell spotted me loitering at the back.

"Come on in, Vincent. It's lovely to see you," she said. I was shocked she even knew who I was as I'd never spoken to her before. I slowly made my way to the front of the hall, my shoes making a scuffing sound against the wooden floor as I walked.

"Take a seat," said Ms Bell.

I headed slowly to one of the chairs and sat down.

"I've got lots of information to hand out about the trip, but I'll wait until everyone gets here," said Ms Bell. As we waited, I got a feeling of hope in my heart. Maybe no one else would turn up? If there wasn't a team of four then the weekend would be cancelled. I felt a small smile of relief spreading across my face, but it quickly faded when I heard the door swing open.

I turned around and saw that it was Lena Kaminski.

"Hello, Lena! Come in, come in," said Ms Bell. "I was just telling Vincent that I'll wait until everyone is here before making a start."

Lena's footsteps echoed around the hall as she made her way over. She sat a few seats away from me, dropping her heavy rucksack by her feet. Her bright blue eyes darted to mine and I looked away. Why had she been invited to take part?

There was a creak as the main door opened again, and Lena and I looked round to see who it was. It was Scarlett Franklin. She stood half-in and half-out of the hall.

"Miss? I've been told I'm supposed to be here, but I don't want to go on the weekend so you can give the place to someone else, OK?" she called.

"Hi, Scarlett. Come on in and sit down, would you?" said Ms Bell, not looking fazed at all.

"But I'm not going," said Scarlett. "So you can just cancel my place. OK?"

Scarlett was incredibly confident and clearly had no intention of going, and I suddenly thought that I should make it known that I wasn't keen either.

"Um. Actually, Ms Bell," I said. "I don't want my place either. Can I go now?"

Ms Bell didn't seem to hear me and looked over at Scarlett. "Come and join us and we can have a little chat about it."

Scarlett rolled her eyes and headed across the hall. She sat next to Lena and huffed so hard that I felt air on my cheek.

"Right, so we are just waiting for one more person," said Ms Bell, looking down at a notepad, although I was pretty sure she could remember four names in her head.

"There's no point me being here, miss," said

Scarlett. "I'm not going, so you need to find someone else."

"The thing is, Scarlett, you've already been confirmed by your parents as a member of the team. It's an incredible opportunity and—"

Ms Bell stopped as the door to the hall crashed open. We all turned round and saw that it was Josh Park, with a big grin on his face.

"Come on, Josh. Don't worry, you're not late! I'm just getting started," said Ms Bell.

"I'm not worried," said Josh. He walked across the hall then tossed his bag on to the floor, slumping into a seat next to Scarlett.

I couldn't believe it. These were the worst people in the world that I could *ever* go away with. THE WORST. How could Mr Hearn think that sending me off on a weekend with these three would be good for me? I'd tell Mum and Dad as soon as I got home that this was most definitely a horrendous mistake.

"Right!" said Ms Bell brightly. "Let's kick things off, shall we? Do you all know each other?"

Scarlett sniffed. "I know her," she said, pointing to Lena. "She's in my form. Her family are into UFOs and weird stuff like that." Lena just stared down at her knees. "And he's in my form too." She pointed to

56

Josh. "But I don't know who he is. Are you new?" she asked me.

I felt my face grow warmer as I shook my head.

"I'm in your form as well," I said quietly.

Scarlett laughed. "No, you're not!" Was I that invisible that she hadn't even noticed me being there?

Ms Bell cleared her throat. "This is the marvellous thing about the Wilderness Warrior Challenge. You will get to find out so much about each other and form really strong bonds," she said.

"I'm not bonding with anyone," said Josh and he began to laugh. He seemed to live in a permanent state of amusement.

Ms Bell ignored him. "So just to confirm that we have Lena, Scarlett, Vincent and Josh. You four have been selected as being students who would benefit the most from going on a weekend such as this. Now, I won't go into the details about why you have been chosen, but what I will do this afternoon is give you some information about what the challenge will entail and a kit list of what you'll need to bring."

Ms Bell got up and handed out the glossy leaflets. I dropped mine on the floor and it scooted over to Scarlett, who put her foot on it. I bent down to get it, but she didn't lift her foot off.

"Can you move your foot, please?" I said.

Scarlett had a sickly sweet smile on her face and just stared at me.

"Scarlett?" said Ms Bell. She shifted her shoe to one side and I grabbed the leaflet and sat down. My heart was thumping. I could feel Scarlett still staring at me and I pretended to be interested in the leaflet. Inside were quotes from students that said things like:

"A life-changing experience!"

"I LOVED it and didn't want it to end!"

"AWESOME!"

"Camping so close to Fortune Mountain was INCREDIBLE. This weekend was the BEST!"

My stomach churned. I glanced at Josh, who was holding his leaflet in one hand and repeatedly tapping it against his leg.

"The Wilderness Warrior Challenge is a weekend consisting of orienteering and camping," said Ms Bell. "You'll cover quite a few miles over the three days, and you'll be cooking your own meals and putting

58

up your tents. There'll be checkpoints throughout so there will always be members of staff on hand to help with any difficulties."

"What's orienteering?" said Josh.

"It's reading maps," said Lena. "I'm quite good at that."

Scarlett raised her eyebrows. "Oh, are you now?" she said. "Came in useful when you went out with Grandpops hunting vampires, did it?"

Lena looked away again and Ms Bell frowned at Scarlett.

"Now, because this trip is coming up in just over a week's time, we are organizing a practice day this Saturday morning on the school field," said Ms Bell, running a hand through her cropped grey hair. "You'll need to come in casual clothes and wear appropriate footwear for all weathers and bring some snacks."

"Can we bring phones?" said Scarlett.

"No, Scarlett. And the only phone allowed on the actual trip will be an emergency mobile that will be in a sealed bag. If you break the seal and use the phone for anything other than an emergency then your team will have failed."

"In that case I vote we break the seal and just get chucked out!" said Josh. "Problem sorted." He grinned at Scarlett who glared back at him.

Lena suddenly sat forward in her seat.

"Ms Bell, is the weekend definitely being held at the Hamlin National Park?" she said. She'd asked about where it was in assembly. What was so fascinating about the area?

"Yes, it is, Lena. Have you been there before?"

Lena shook her head. "No, but I've heard of it."

"Well, I think you'll love it. I've cycled around there and it's an area of outstanding natural beauty. The views are incredible. Especially the panorama of Fortune Mountain," said Ms Bell with a huge grin on her face. She handed out some more pieces of paper.

"This sheet gives you all the information you will need about what kit to bring. You'll need a roomy rucksack, a decent pair of walking books, some good quality socks, an all-weather sleeping bag and a basic first-aid kit. The school will provide the tents, ground mats and camping equipment."

Ms Bell directed the next part at Josh.

"I think the school have spoken to your parents about your kit, Josh."

Josh's permanent grin disintegrated into a look of embarrassment. Everyone knew that his family struggled a bit – just like so many other families in school – but I wasn't sure that it was nice for Ms Bell to comment on it in front of us.

"On Saturday morning, Mr Hearn and I will show you how to put up your tents, read a map and use the camping stoves. Won't that be great? To learn some life skills?"

She looked at each of us in turn. Scarlett was still slumped in her seat looking utterly miserable, Lena was clutching her rucksack in her lap and was clearly ready to go home, and Josh was picking something off the bottom of his shoe.

"Are there any questions?" said Ms Bell.

I swallowed. No one said anything and then Scarlett spoke.

"What do I need to do to get out of it?" she said. "I don't want to go."

This was exactly the thing I wanted to ask.

"OK, Scarlett. I think I already know how much you don't want to go, but your form tutor and, in fact, all of your teachers, think that you'd really benefit from getting away and spending some time with some other students for a change."

Scarlett looked at me, Josh and Lena. "Great," she said sarcastically.

"Are there any more questions?" said Ms Bell. We

all remained silent. "Good! Then I'll see you bright and early on Saturday morning, if not before."

Lena jumped out of her seat and jogged towards the door. I got up and tripped on a chair leg and stumbled. I heard Scarlett laugh.

I hurried across the hall and through the heavy door, letting it slam behind me.

This was a complete and utter disaster.

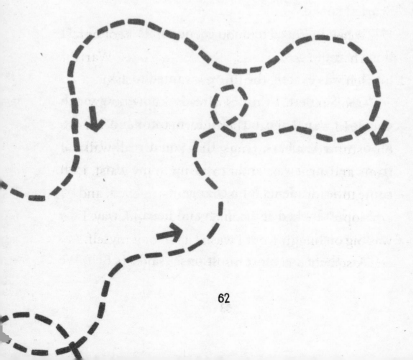

Chapter Eight

Painful Boots

Dad's car was parked on our drive when I got home.

"Ah ha! Here he is, the Wilderness Warrior himself!" said Dad, coming out of the kitchen.

I took my shoes off and dumped them by the stairs. In the hallway there were two large carrier bags stuffed with camping gear, a pair of grey walking boots and a rucksack that came up to my waist. Dad came towards me with his arms outstretched, and he enveloped me before I could get out of the way. Dad was big on hugging but I wasn't a fan of it myself. My cheek squished against his fleece jumper.

"Where's Mum?" I asked, my voice muffled.

"She's gone into town with Ewan."

At least I had Dad on his own for a change.

"So? Tell me all. How was the Wilderness Warriors meeting?"

"Not good," I said. I ducked out of the hug and went to the kitchen.

"I'm sure it wasn't that bad," he said, following me. "And remember we only use positive language in this house. OK?"

I thought about pointing out to him that this wasn't actually his house any more so I could say what I wanted, but I picked up an apple from the fruit bowl and bit into that instead.

"I've brought a few bits and pieces over so you'll be all set and ready for the challenge," said Dad. "Wait there!" He went back to the hall and returned with the bags and the boots.

"These took Ewan up Snowdon *and* Ben Nevis," said Dad, waving the boots at me. "They've still got some miles in them yet."

He plonked them on to the floor.

"And in here we have a couple of sleeping bags, a water bottle, gloves, waterproof trousers and some other bits."

He grinned at me but I already felt overwhelmed with all the things I was supposed to pack. I was going to lose so much stuff, I just knew it.

"There are also high quality walking socks in there. People think that you just need good boots but you also need decent socks. Ones that will let your feet breathe."

I tried to summon some excitement about socks but I just couldn't manage it. I finished the apple and threw the core towards the food recycling bin, missing it by miles.

"Come on. Let's try the boots on for size, shall we?" said Dad.

He pulled out a chair. I thought about refusing, but Dad looked so happy that I found myself sitting down. Although I didn't want to go on the trip, it was nice that Dad was so enthusiastic about something to do with me for a change. I slipped my feet into the boots. They felt big and clumpy. I tried to tie the red laces, but this kind of thing is hard when you have dyspraxia. Dad saw me struggling and kneeled down to tie them for me. I felt like a five-year-old.

"We can change these laces for those magnetic clip ones you like," he said. I had some of those on my trainers and they just snap together. They were much easier. Dad did a final knot and got up.

"Right. Have a little stroll. Get a feel for them."

I stood up and walked around the kitchen. The one on the right foot was OK, but the one on my left rubbed against my heel.

"They're a bit uncomfortable," I said.

Dad frowned. "I don't see how they can be, Vincent. They are one of the best brands you can get. They're waterproof too."

I walked around the table and sat down. I thought that the boots had probably moulded to Ewan's foot shape and not mine and that was why they felt weird. Dad went to the hall again and came back with the rucksack.

"Ta-da!" he said. "Look at this! Isn't it fab?"

On the rucksack were a variety of sewn-on felt badges. I spotted one that said *Three-Peak Challenge* and another that showed a silhouette of a person hanging by their fingertips from an overhanging rock. Ewan must have collected them from his various trips.

"Let's see how it fits, shall we?" said Dad. He held the rucksack up like a coat, waiting for me to slip it on. I put my arms through the straps, and Dad immediately began to tug and tighten various parts of the rucksack. He snapped a clasp around my chest and did up another one that stretched around my stomach. I didn't realize that carrying a bag could be so complicated, and I was already dreading how I'd get the thing off.

"How does it feel?" he said, stepping back and studying me. The weight of it was pulling me backwards.

"It's really heavy," I said. "What's in it?"

Dad rubbed at his chin. "It's empty, Vincent. It's literally just the rucksack."

"What?!" I said. "I can't carry this *and* all the stuff that I need to take. It'll be too much!"

I fiddled with the clasps but I couldn't undo them. I began to tug on the straps instead. But the more I tugged the tighter they became.

"Get it off me!" I shouted.

"Calm down, Vincent," said Dad. "There's no need to panic."

Dad easily popped one of the clasps open and I managed to shimmy out of one arm. I pulled the rucksack off and threw it on the floor. Then I undid the laces of the boots the best I could, tugged them off and I threw them on top of the bag.

"There is absolutely NO POINT in me doing this trip," I said. "I can't even take the rucksack off! *Or* do my laces up! I'll just end up losing stuff or leaving it behind."

Dad sighed. "Don't be ridiculous, Vincent. We'll sort out everything you need to take. This is an amazing opportunity and—"

"No, Dad. It's NOT an amazing opportunity. I'm NOT interested in this kind of thing. You just want me to do it because it's the sort of thing you and Ewan like to do. Not me!"

I'd never spoken to my dad like that before, and I felt a bit stunned that the words had come out of my mouth. I stared at him to see how he was going to react. He was silent for moment and then he sat down.

"I get it, Vincent. I really do," he said. "You don't need to be ashamed to admit that you're scared."

"I'm NOT scared," I said. "I just don't want to go! Why can't you and Mum understand?"

I put my arms on to the table and hid my face so he couldn't see me. I *was* scared. But there was no way I was going to tell Dad that. And the thought of being stuck with those other kids also filled me with dread. Especially when they saw how useless I was. I heard Dad picking up the rucksack and boots.

"OK, Vincent," he said. "I'll talk to your mum when she gets back, and we'll send an email to the school and say that you won't be going after all. They'll have to find another student to take your place."

I looked up.

"Really?" I said.

Dad nodded. "Yep. We won't push you."

"Thank you," I said. I wiped my nose. I couldn't quite believe it was this easy, but I didn't say anything in case he changed his mind.

"You can just carry on as you are and nothing will change," said Dad.

I thought about the years ahead of me that I still had in school, rushing from class to class in the hope that no one would notice me.

"Um," I said, "and you'll tell Mr Hearn and Ms Bell?"

"Yes," said Dad. "We'll tell them that you're not quite ready for this kind of challenge. I'll go and put everything back in the car."

He turned away and I noticed that his shoulders seemed to have dropped and his head hung down as he walked out. I felt a little guilty but I was too relieved to feel that bad.

I heard the front door open. Mum and Ewan were home. Dad and Mum were mumbling in the hallway and I imagined Dad was telling her how everything had changed and that I wasn't going after all.

Ewan came into the kitchen and went straight to the cupboard for a chocolate bar.

"All right?" he said, tearing the wrapper and taking a huge bite. He leaned against the counter.

"Yeah," I said. I got up to get a drink.

"When's your trip?" said Ewan. "I'm well jealous."

I filled up a glass of water and had a sip.

"I'm not going," I said. "Dad's going to email the school tonight."

Ewan stuffed the rest of the bar in his mouth.

"Why's that, then?" said Ewan.

I shrugged. "Don't want to," I said.

Ewan scrunched up the wrapper and effortlessly lobbed it into the bin.

"My mate Tomasz said his sister is in your year and she's going on the trip too. Lena. Do you know her?" said Ewan.

I nodded.

"She's absolutely terrified apparently," said Ewan.

"Really?" I said. She hadn't seemed scared at

the meeting, but maybe she was good at hiding her feelings. "Why is she doing it, then?"

"I don't know. Tomasz said that some girls keep being mean to her at school. I think she's had quite a rough time."

I thought about the times I'd seen Lena getting picked on by Scarlett, Melanie and Holly, and I wondered how she felt about Scarlett being one of the team.

"And she thinks that going on this weekend is going to stop the other girls being horrible to her?" I said.

Ewan found a currant bun in our bread bin. He was constantly eating.

"I don't know, but I think she sounds really brave, to be honest. Tomasz said they are all proud of her for going."

I gulped down some water. I guessed Mum and Dad wouldn't be so proud of me any more.

"Listen, Vincent, I know Dad can be a bit full-on sometimes, but he's usually right about this kind of stuff." He shoved the remainder of the currant bun in his mouth. "I think you should go. Prove to yourself that you can do it." He pushed himself away from the kitchen counter. "Right, I gotta go or I'll be late for quad biking. See ya later."

I sat down at the table and thought about how scared Lena must be about this trip. I might have no friends but at least I wasn't getting hassled by anyone. Dad came back into the kitchen with his car keys in his hand.

"I'm off now, Vincent," he said. "I've spoken to your mum and I'm going to email the school tonight and let them know that you won't be going."

I nodded. "OK," I said. Dad sighed, then walked away.

So, it was all decided. The Wilderness Warriors Challenge was over before it had even begun. I was expecting to feel like an almighty weight had been lifted from my shoulders.

But I just felt like I was somehow letting myself down.

That evening I went into Ewan's old bedroom to play *Battle Doom*. It was a relief to do something to take my mind off the challenge, but even in my game everything seemed to go wrong. I was trying to investigate the old well in the village of Brunfawn. I had a feeling that there was something important down there – possibly even the diamond itself. But the annoying travelling hawker was back – the one who was insisting on selling me something. He kept blocking my way. I was certain he was trying to distract me so that he could rob me, so I used my last sleeping potion on him. Then I tried to climb into the well, but Fabian lost his grip and plummeted downwards, ending the game. I went back to my saved point and tried again. But it happened every single time. He clearly could go down the well – the game wouldn't allow him to go so far if it wasn't possible – but he just seemed to give up.

I watched as Fabian fell one more time and big white graphics came on to the screen:

GAME OVER

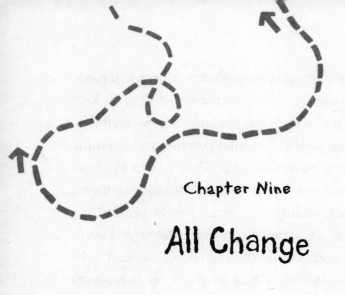

Chapter Nine

All Change

When I got to school the next day, I hurried across the playground to stand near the science block. There was a path there that was always deserted and not out of bounds, so it was one of my favourite places to hang around. There were a few minutes to go until the bell went for registration. I fumbled in my bag and took out my school planner so that I had something to look at while I was waiting. The crumpled leaflet that Ms Bell had handed out for the Wilderness Warriors Challenge fell out, and I bent to get it.

"Hi, Vincent," said a voice. I stood up. It was Lena.

"Hi," I said.

"Are you looking forward to the weekend too?" she asked. She spotted the leaflet in my hand and must have thought I was reading it.

"Oh. No. I'm not going," I said. I stuffed the leaflet into my blazer pocket.

Lena looked puzzled.

"What do you mean?" she asked.

I shrugged. "I didn't want to do it, so my parents are telling the school I don't have to go."

Lena blinked quickly and looked away across the playground. I wasn't certain but it looked a bit like she had tears in her eyes.

"B-but you have to come," she said. "I can't go with just Scarlett and Josh. It'll be *awful*."

"Yeah, and that's why I'm not going. The whole thing is going to be a disaster. Just tell your parents you don't want to do it," I said. While I fumbled with my bag I dropped my planner and Lena quickly picked it up and handed it to me.

"But I *want* to go, Vincent," she said. "It's important to me."

I wondered why on earth it was so important to her, but I shook my head. "Sorry," I said.

75

The bell went for registration and I hurried off to form time.

Mr Hearn didn't say anything to me about the challenge at registration. I guessed he was probably disappointed with me as well.

My first lesson was geography and, for some reason, Josh decided that it would be funny to make a noise like a dripping tap by flicking the side of his cheek. We'd all seen and heard him do it countless times before, and it had stopped being even slightly amusing months ago. Every time our teacher, Mr Drake, turned around to see what the noise was, Josh stopped.

"Can anyone hear that?" said Mr Drake. No one said anything and Mr Drake looked up at the ceiling to see if there was some kind of leak. When he couldn't find anything, he shrugged and turned back to the whiteboard. I looked over at Josh as he took a small scrap of paper and rolled it into a small ball. He lobbed it across the room and it hit Melanie on the back of the head. She turned around with a scowl on her face but couldn't tell where it had come from. Josh's face was red from trying not to laugh out loud. He didn't seem to realize that he was the only one who found it amusing.

"Mr Park, is there something you want to share with the class?" said Mr Drake, spotting Josh messing around at last.

Josh pretended to think about it.

"Yes," he said. "I'd like to share that I don't like geography as it's really boring."

He looked around the class for everyone to join in laughing, but no one did.

Mr Drake began to fold the sleeves of his shirt up, which usually meant he was about to get angry.

"If you find it so boring you can go and report to the office. Out you go, Josh," said Mr Drake. "Tell them I sent you. Again."

I noticed Josh's fixed grin falter a little, but he got his stuff together and walked out.

At lunchtime I sat in a corner of the canteen and took out my packed lunch. It was always noisy with the sound of everyone chatting and laughing together. I hated it. I'd tried to sit with people in the past and join in, but it just got me some strange looks and made me feel really uncomfortable. It was like everyone else was in some exclusive club and I was the only person in the year who wasn't a member.

I spotted Lena at a table not far from where I was

sitting. Scarlett, Melanie and Holly surrounded her and Scarlett peered into Lena's lunchbox.

"Urgh. What is that?" she said loudly. "Is that Polish? Do you actually eat that stuff?"

Lena kept her head down and nodded. She said something, probably telling Scarlett what the food was called, but Scarlett began to make retching noises and pretended to put her fingers down her throat. Melanie and Holly thought it was hilarious.

Lena caught my eye and I quickly looked away.

"Hey. There's a five-a-side going on on the astro pitch. Wanna be on our team?" yelled a voice.

I looked up from my sandwich and saw that it was a boy called Miles. He was looking in my direction but his eyes were on someone else.

"Yeah. See you there in a bit," said a girl's voice behind me.

My heart sank a little, even though I would have said no if he'd been asking me. Footballs and me don't mix.

I glanced back up at Lena. Scarlett was sitting really close to her, eating some kind of pasta bolognese that was being served in the cafeteria. She got a spoonful then dropped it right into Lena's lunchbox.

"There you go," she said. "Have something actually edible for a change, eh?"

Lena just stared down at her lunch and wiped at her cheek. Before I realized what I was doing, I had stuffed my remaining lunch into my bag and was walking over to her table.

"Hi, Lena," I said. Scarlett, Melanie and Holly all glared at me with narrowed eyes. "Hi, Vincent," said Lena. She looked up at me, eager for help.

"Oh, you're the other one going on the trip, aren't you?" said Scarlett, slumping back in her seat. "So that makes the weirdo, the invisible boy and the clown. Terrific."

Lena was frowning at me. Probably waiting for me to say how I wasn't actually going any more. But I found myself holding my head a little higher.

"Yes. I am," I said. I turned to Lena. "Do you fancy going to the library?"

Lena's face was beaming and she quickly stood up. "Sure," she said.

"Can you believe I've actually got to go away with those saddos?" Scarlett said to Melanie and Holly. "It's going to be *awful*."

We could hear them laughing across the canteen as we walked away.

"You *are* coming!" said Lena. "That's brilliant!"

"It looks like it," I said. I was regretting it already.

Could I go back on what I'd just said? After all, I still *really* didn't want to go. And I'd have to let the school know and tell Mum and Dad. Surely they'd all be angry about being messed around?

The corridor that led to the library was really busy and I kept knocking into people. I accidentally smacked into a boy in Year Nine. He quickly spun round.

"Oi, watch it!" he sneered.

"Sorry," I muttered. Lena stepped in front of me and I followed her. It was like she was clearing the way so that I didn't bump into anyone else. But no pupils in school knew about my dyspraxia so it was probably just coincidence.

We got to the library and I went to the desk to return my book even though I hadn't even taken it out of my bag. Library books were just part of my ammunition against being lonely, like Fabian used bows and arrows against his foes.

I looked to see where Lena had gone and saw that she had put her bag on a table and was running her finger along the spines of the books in the history section. She took a book from the shelf titled: *Undiscovered Historical Artefacts.*

"Is that for homework?" I asked.

She jumped. "No. I just thought I'd do a bit of reading. I'll see you later, Vincent." She turned to face the books again, and I stood there for a moment, confused and a bit crushed. For a moment I'd thought I had someone to hang out in the library with for a change. But she clearly had other ideas. She took the book from the shelf and sat down at a desk, getting out a notebook. What was she doing? I headed to the door, thinking where I could head next to kill some time.

When I got home after school I told Mum, very reluctantly, that I would go on the Wilderness Warriors Challenge after all. She gave a little 'whoop' and said she'd ring the school immediately and that I should call Dad and let him know.

Dad sounded pretty emotional when I told him.

"Can I just say how proud I am of you for stepping up to the mark?" he said. "It takes a strong person to know their weaknesses. And an even stronger one to face up to them."

I wasn't entirely sure what he was getting at and it sounded a little bit insulting, but I still said; "Thanks, Dad."

Chapter Ten

Practice Day Disaster

Mum drove me to school on Saturday morning for our Wilderness Warriors practice session. My school rucksack was between my feet containing my drink and snacks, not that I could imagine being able to stomach anything. I felt sick inside and I'd only managed to nibble half a slice of toast for breakfast. What if this morning was awful? How would I get through a whole weekend?

We pulled up outside the school and Mum twisted round to face me.

"You'll be fine, Vincent," she said. "It'll be a good

chance for you to get to know your teammates before the actual weekend, won't it? Oh, look. Is that one of them arriving now?"

A large silver car pulled up and Scarlett got out. She was wearing a short denim jacket over a pink T-shirt with tight black leggings and a pair of bright white trainers. Her glossy brown hair was curled and cascaded down her back. As she turned I saw that her eyebrows had been coloured in and they were black and knitted together in a deep frown. She slammed the car door and stomped across the school car park.

"She looks friendly!" said Mum.

"She's the worst girl in the whole school, Mum. She's a bully," I said.

Mum frowned. "Is she nasty to you? Because if she is, I'll go and—"

"No. Not me. But she has got it in for a girl in my form." I imagined how awful Lena must be feeling right now.

The driver's door of the silver car opened up and a glamorous woman got out.

"SCARLETT!" she screeched.

Scarlett stopped and turned around.

"DON'T EAT TOO MANY OF THOSE BISCUITS

OR THEY'LL MAKE YOUR TEETH ROT!" she yelled. "AND DON'T RUIN THOSE TRAINERS!"

I waited for Scarlett to scream something in reply, but instead she just nodded and walked away. Her mum got back into her car and sped off.

Mum looked at me and raised her eyebrows.

"Remember it finishes at one o'clock," I said. "Don't be late, will you?" I didn't want to stay there one second longer than I had to. I wanted to get home and play *Battle Doom* again.

"I won't. I promise," said Mum. "Now. Off you go and have *fun*."

I grabbed my rucksack and headed towards Scarlett, who was standing by reception and scrolling on her phone. I had no idea where we were supposed to be meeting so I was at least grateful that someone else was here. Ewan's left boot felt like sandpaper against my heel and I wriggled it as I walked, trying to make it less painful.

"Hi, Scarlett," I said, standing next to her. "Do you know where we are supposed to go?"

She looked up and seemed surprised to see me. I waited for her to make another snide comment about me being invisible or something.

"No," she said, and then she went back to her phone.

I took a few steps away, waiting to see if anyone would appear to tell us what to do. Just when I was beginning to feel even more uncomfortable, Mr Hearn trotted round the corner from the direction of the school field.

"Hi, Vincent. Hi, Scarlett," he said. He was wearing matching blue joggers and sweatshirt with a grey baseball cap with *AIM HIGH* written on it in silver. It was all very different from his usual black trousers and white shirt.

"Whoa, sir," said Scarlett, taking him in. "You look … casual."

Mr Hearn grinned, taking off the cap and wiping a palm across his receding hairline.

"Why, thank you, Scarlett," he said, even though it wasn't exactly a compliment. "We're just setting up on the field, so, Scarlett, I suggest you put your phone in your bag and don't get it out until we are finished. OK?"

Scarlett carried on typing for a few seconds and then put the phone into her bag with a coordinated eye roll.

As we walked to the field, Mr Hearn asked us about our camping experiences.

"Have either of you slept in a tent before?" he said.

I shook my head. I'd been camping just the once on the school field when I was in primary school. I couldn't sleep and the teacher had to ring my mum at one a.m. to come and get me as I was getting upset. So technically, no, I hadn't slept in a tent.

"Absolutely not," said Scarlett. "What's the point when you've got houses and stuff?" I had to agree with her on that one. Her comment seemed to stop Mr Hearn's conversation in its tracks, and he didn't say a great deal after that.

When we got to the field, Ms Bell was there with Lena.

"Good morning, you two! Isn't this brilliant?" said Ms Bell, looking like she was about to explode from the excitement. "When Josh arrives we'll start. OK?"

Scarlett sniffed and I nodded. There were some large blue bundles on the grass which I guessed were the tents. I hoped they weren't going to be too complicated.

I looked over at Lena. She was wearing a pair of orange-and-black walking boots and some khaki-coloured trousers with zipped pockets in the legs. She looked like a professional hiker.

"Ah, and here comes Josh," said Mr Hearn. "Hi, Josh!"

Josh looked like he was off to the beach, wearing a football T-shirt, some long frayed denim shorts and flip-flops.

"All right?" he said, plonking himself straight on to the grass.

"Morning, Josh," said Ms Bell, staring at his feet for a few seconds. She must have decided not to mention his choice of 'appropriate footwear' as she carried on. "OK. Mr Hearn and I are going to demonstrate how to put up a tent and then you'll be working in pairs to put up your own. You'll have two tents between the four of you. One for the girls and one for the boys."

This was getting worse. I'd have to share a tent with Josh?!

"Can I have my own tent?" said Scarlett. "I'm not sharing."

She glanced at Lena, who was looking at Ms Bell.

"No, Scarlett. And you'll be grateful I said that as you really won't want to carry any extra weight on the day. Right. Shall we get started, Eamon? I mean, Mr Hearn?"

"Yes!" said Mr Hearn, slapping his hands together. "Let's show you how easy it is."

He took the tent out of a canvas bag and unrolled it on the ground. Then he showed us some peg things and also some poles that fitted together to make long sticks, some string things called guy ropes and another piece of tarpaulin that was a ground sheet. Within about twenty minutes the whole thing was put together and Ms Bell was inside, demonstrating how to zip up the front.

"And that's all there is to it!" said Mr Hearn. "Josh? Up you get now. And, Vincent? Here is your tent." He picked up one of the large blue bundles and threw it towards me. It hit me in the stomach and I immediately dropped it. "And this is yours, Lena and Scarlett." Lena caught hers and walked over to where there was a bit more space.

"We'll help you if necessary, but let's see how you get on first. Off you go," said Mr Hearn.

Josh slowly got to his feet and then he just stared at me.

"Right," I said, trying to sound confident. "I guess let's get it out of the bag."

I shook the contents on to the ground, and we both stared at the pile of stuff.

"Well, go on, then," said Josh, grinning. "Put it up."

I kneeled down and tried to remember what everything was. Josh just stood there with his arms folded. I looked over at Ms Bell and Mr Hearn to see if they might step in and tell him to help, but they were busy talking.

Forty minutes later and our tent was still flat on the ground. Josh had sat down and was picking at the grass. I looked over at the girls. They were both at least trying to work it out together and their tent had got some shape to it, but with every gust of wind it kept lifting off the ground.

"Arrghh, this is so POINTLESS!" yelled Scarlett as the middle of their tent collapsed.

I unfolded one of the snappy poles and attempted to feed it through a little fabric hole.

"I'm not being funny, mate, but aren't you one of those brainy kids who does everything right all the time?" said Josh. "You don't seem to be that smart, to be honest."

"Maybe you could help me, then?" I snapped.

"Nah, you're all right," said Josh, leaning back on to his elbow.

I could feel tears starting to sting my eyes. For me, attempting anything like this was my worst nightmare. Twenty minutes later Ms Bell and Mr Hearn finally stepped in.

"OK. We can see that you're struggling a bit so we're going to help you finish up."

Mr Hearn helped the girls and Ms Bell came over to us. She talked through everything that she was doing, but I found it difficult to keep up. Josh was now lying flat on his back, staring up at the clouds.

"Josh? You should be watching this. It's not just Vincent's responsibility, you know," said Ms Bell. "You need to work together. Remember, this is a competition and the other teams will be well-practised."

"Yeah. I'm watching," said Josh, clearly not.

At last both of the tents were up and Mr Hearn checked his watch.

"That's taken a little longer than we anticipated, so I think the next thing we need to show you is how to use your cooking equipment. After all, these are the two most important basic survival skills – building a shelter and feeding yourself."

I was also keen to learn the skill of 'how not to die on a walking trip with people who hate each other', but maybe that would be covered in a later lesson.

Ms Bell dragged over a box containing the cooking equipment and placed a small camping stove on to the ground. She showed us how to light it, and then she boiled up some water in something called a billycan to make us all a hot chocolate. Josh didn't show any interest until his drink was ready, but at least Lena and Scarlett were both watching. We sat on the ground outside our tents and drank the hot chocolate out of enamel mugs. I burned my tongue on the first sip and it didn't taste of anything after that. We got our snacks out. Josh didn't have anything with him so Mr Hearn gave him one of his ginger biscuits. I looked at my watch and was relieved to see that we only had an hour left.

"Well, this is nice, isn't it?" said Mr Hearn. "You can't beat the glorious outdoors."

"Sir, it's the school field," said Josh through a mouthful of biscuit.

Lena cleared her throat. She hadn't said a great deal all day. I wondered if knowing she'd have to share a tent with Scarlett had stunned her into silence.

"Will we be getting a map of the area where we'll be walking?" she said.

"Ah! I'm glad you asked that, Lena, because that is going to be our next exercise," said Mr Hearn. He reached for a plastic folder beside him.

"This pack contains everything you need. Using a compass and a waterproof map, you will need to work out a route that will take you to each checkpoint along the course."

He unfolded the map and placed it on the ground in the middle of us. Josh leaned forward and looked at it, then began to laugh.

"How are we supposed to read that?" he said. "It's just a load of lines and squiggles!"

Scarlett looked too. "There are no roads or anything!"

"You'll be travelling across open countryside, Scarlett. That is the point of the challenge," said Ms Bell.

"We'll just use Google Maps," said Josh. "Sorted!"

"We're not allowed phones," said Lena.

Ms Bell went on to explain how to read a map using coordinates and a compass, but she was going quite quickly and I didn't understand everything she was saying. Lena kept nodding, and I hoped her comment about knowing how to read a map at the meeting was true. Scarlett and Josh didn't even bother to pretend that they were listening.

At one o'clock our practice session was finished and we still hadn't covered everything.

"Right, that's all we have time for today," said Ms Bell, folding up the map while Mr Hearn packed all of the tents away, miraculously squeezing everything into the little bags. "Who wants to take the map and start thinking about the route?"

"I will," said Lena. She took the map and began to look at it closely. It reminded me of her staring intently at the book in the library.

"This week, remember to make sure you have everything you need from the kit list. And you'll need to get together and decide what food you want to bring."

"Baked beans!" said Josh, and he made a farting noise.

"We'll have another run-through in school on Friday lunchtime. Before then I suggest the four of you get together in your own time to discuss food and how you plan to share out those extra bits. I think that's all we can cover today."

Scarlett got up and took her phone out of her bag. "Can I go now?" she said. Ms Bell nodded and she stormed off across the field. I noticed that her white trainers were streaked with grass stains. I got up and followed too.

My feet were in shreds and my tongue was still burning from the hot chocolate.

I couldn't wait to get home to play *Battle Doom* and forget all about it.

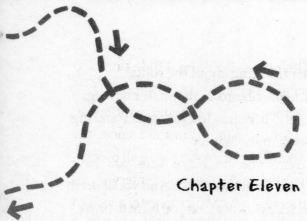

Chapter Eleven

An Ultimate Failure

On Sunday afternoon it was Ewan's football club's end-of-season presentation. This was a yearly event involving boring speeches and us watching a gazillion trophies being handed out to loads of teams. I asked Mum if I could stay at home so that I could play *Battle Doom*. (Obviously I told her that it was so I could do my homework). She said no and that it would be nice for me to be there for my brother. She seemed to forget that I spent most of my life 'being there' for my brother. Football pitches, swimming pools, basketball courts, windsurfing lakes... I'd been to them all. I knew he was brilliant at everything. I didn't need to watch him get yet another trophy.

We walked into the hall at the club and found a seat. I spotted the back of Ewan's head in the second row from the front. He and his teammates were all dressed smartly like they were waiting for a job interview or something. On the stage was a microphone, a lectern and a table packed with loads of golden trophies. I groaned. It would take hours to get through all of those!

Dad waved at us and came over. He gave Mum a kiss on her cheek and squeezed my shoulder. He looked nervous, as if he was up for an award too.

"I'm not sure if he's going to win the triple again, but we can only hope," said Dad. The 'triple' meant the three main trophies for each team, voted for by different people: players' player, manager's player and spectators' player of the year.

Mum wriggled out of her jacket. "Can you imagine if he wins two years running?" They both grinned.

"I'll go and check how he's doing," said Dad.

"Tell him good luck from us!" said Mum. Dad crossed his fingers, then headed off towards where Ewan was sitting.

"How long is this going to go on for?" I asked. Although I already knew the answer: for ever.

"I'm sure it won't be hours," said Mum. But it was. We sat there for so long my bum went completely numb. Obviously, Ewan won the triple. Mum started crying and stood up to clap but I stayed in my seat. After it was over, Mum and I went back to Dad's house for a 'celebratory barbecue'.

When we got there we walked around the side of the house straight into the garden. Dad was in his navy-and-white striped apron and holding some metal tongs. He'd already got the barbecue going and was about to put some burgers on the grill.

"Let's hope the weather stays like this for your weekend, eh, Vincent?" said Dad. "Not too hot and not too cold. That's the perfect walking weather, that is."

I was hoping that, with all the attention being on Ewan, I would escape any Wilderness Warriors chat. No such luck.

Ewan came through the kitchen door with a jug of lemonade and some plastic beakers.

Mum went over and gave him a big kiss.

"I'm so proud of you!" she said. Ewan just shrugged. On the patio was a table laid with plates, cutlery, salad and bread. I noticed that Ewan's trophies were on the table too and I picked one up and had a look at it. It was a golden figure of a footballer about to kick a ball. Underneath was a little plaque with Ewan's name.

"Isn't this exactly the same trophy that they gave out last year?" I asked. I was trying to bring him down a bit, I guess. Ewan just laughed. "Yeah. It is," he said. "They probably buy a job lot!"

I sat down and then I spotted a rolled-up tent lying on the lawn; my heart sank. Ewan saw where I was looking.

"I thought you'd like to have a practice putting it up!" he said. "It's always good to be as prepared as possible."

He really was morphing into Dad.

"I'm fine, thanks," I said.

Mum poured the lemonade.

"There's no harm in having a go," said Mum. "I'm sure Ewan will help you if you get stuck."

"I don't want to," I said quietly.

Mum sighed, then got up to take a drink over to Dad.

I knew exactly what would happen if I tried to put up the tent. I'd get in a muddle and not be able to do the fiddly stuff, then Ewan would butt in and take over, making me feel completely incapable. He might be brilliant at everything but he had zero patience.

For Ewan's twelfth birthday he'd had a party at an indoor assault course called The Ultimate Obstacle. It was like a giant soft-play centre, but for much older kids and adults. I was eight at the time and really excited to be joining in with his special evening. At the start there was a safety talk from one of the staff and then we went to the lockers to take off our shoes. Ewan spotted me and came over with a big scowl on his face.

"You won't be able to do it, Vincent," he said. "Just watch with Mum and Dad, OK?"

I was gobsmacked. All along I'd thought I was going to be taking part!

"But why?" I said. "I want to have a go too!" I could already see some of the course which involved clambering up soft square blocks and crawling through tunnels. It looked brilliant.

"Mum! Tell him!" yelled Ewan. Mum came over.

"Your brother is just worried you'll find it a bit tricky, Vincent," said Mum. "Why don't we get an ice cream and we can watch from the cafe?"

"NO!" I shouted.

Dad came over and put a hand on my shoulder.

"I think Vincent should have a go if he wants to," he said. Ewan shot daggers at Dad and stormed off to his friends. I was thrilled!

"Just take it steady, Vincent. You don't have to try and keep up with the older boys," said Mum.

Ewan and his three friends were called forward to the start and I stood with them, waiting.

"Remember we've got to stay together," Ewan said to the group. A hooter sounded and we were off. Ewan and his friends raced to climb a rope wall that went up to the top of a huge pink slide. I ran to join them. I struggled to get my foot into the first rung, but everyone else scampered up to the top.

"Come on, Vincent!" Ewan yelled down to me.

It was hard, slow work, but I got to the top eventually and grinned at my big brother.

"I did it!" I said.

Ewan wasn't smiling.

"Just don't be so slow, OK? We're supposed to stay together." He zoomed down the slide into a massive ball pool and I followed. I waded across to the edge and had a bit of trouble pulling myself out.

"Can you help me out, Ewan?" I said. But my brother shook his head.

"I've got to catch the others up!" he said, and he ran off.

I got out and crawled into a purple tunnel. The whoops and squeals of Ewan and his friends echoed around me as they exited at the other end. I emerged to face a pit filled with large foam squares and rectangles. Dangling in front of me was a rope. Ewan and his three friends were on the other side. At least they'd waited for me.

"You've got to swing across, Vincent!" he shouted. "If you fall in you've got to try again."

I hesitated. This looked really hard. I took hold of the rope and leaped off of the side, but I lost my grip and fell.

"He's never going to do it," I heard one of his friends say. "Come on, let's go."

The foam pieces were really hard to get over and I struggled to the side and climbed out. I took the rope again.

"You've got to gain more momentum to get across or you won't make it," shouted Ewan. "Don't let go!" He was on his own now because his friends had carried on without him.

I swallowed and held the rope tightly. I took a step back then launched myself for a second time. I dangled in mid-air, but I wasn't close enough to get across. I tried to flex my body to make myself move but it was too hard and I dropped into the pit.

"Can't I just climb out on your side?" I said.

"NO, VINCENT!" said Ewan, getting more

agitated. "That's not the point, is it? You've *got* to complete the obstacles! Hurry up!"

I tried one more time but the rope was burning my hands and I fell in again.

One of Ewan's friends suddenly reappeared, flushed and sweaty.

"Come on, Ewan. He's spoiling the whole thing. Just leave him!" he said, before running off. Ewan looked at me.

"I told you that you couldn't do it!" he said. And then he rushed off to join his friends.

I started to cry. I was tired, I was snotty and my brother had left me. Eventually one of the staff came over and helped me out, taking me to a special exit where Mum and Dad were waiting.

"Don't worry, Vincent. At least you had a go, eh?" said Dad.

"If I wasn't so *clumsy* I would have been able to do it," I sobbed.

"Oh, Vincent. I'm sure it's got nothing to do with your dyspraxia. You're just a bit too young, that's all," said Mum.

I didn't care what the reason was. All I knew was that, yet again, I was useless at something and my brother was better.

On the way home, Ewan made it clear how embarrassing it was that I couldn't keep up and how his friends had found it annoying. While Dad told Ewan that not everyone could be good at everything, I stared out of the window. It must have been frustrating for Ewan – to have a brother who couldn't join in like him – but as I sat in the back of the car, I'd decided I'd never try to do something in front of my brother ever again.

"The burgers are ready!" called Dad, snapping me out of my daydream. "Bring your plates over, guys."

I went over to the barbecue with a bun on a plate.

"You are going to love cooking outside on your trip," said Dad, flipping the burgers over, then choosing one for me. I held out my plate and he placed the burger inside my bun.

"I think food always tastes better when it's cooked on an open fire. Don't you, Ewan?" said Dad.

"Oh, for sure!" said Ewan.

I walked slowly back towards the table, but the burger began to slide on my plate. I tilted it upright, but I didn't see the rolled-up tent and I tripped, catapulting my burger into the air. I managed to stay standing, but the burger landed on the grass and I trod straight on it with my trainer.

"Whoa!" called Ewan. "Burger overboard!"

I looked at Ewan. He was laughing, his cheeks bulging with food. Dad was beside him grinning, and Mum was smiling with her hand on the top of her head. The three of them looked so amused. I felt anger bubbling inside of me.

"What did you leave the tent there for?!" I yelled.

Ewan looked shocked. "I didn't think you'd trip over it, Vincent. It wasn't in the way."

He was right. Because I'd been concentrating so hard on not dropping my plate, I'd veered away from the table a bit.

"It's all right for you, isn't it? You never do *anything* wrong," I shouted.

"Vincent," said Dad. "Come on. Just give your brother a hug, eh?"

"No, Dad. I don't *want* a hug," I said. "I *hate* hugging. Haven't you ever noticed?"

I looked at Mum and Dad's faces. They looked horrified.

I went to kick the burger but my foot missed.

"See? I can't even get that right!" I said. Then I stomped off inside and hid in the downstairs toilet.

*

Mum and I left not long after the burger incident. When I came out of the toilet, I'd noticed that Ewan's trophies had disappeared from the table and the tent had also vanished.

Dad kept looking at me, and I knew he wanted to talk about what had just happened, but I think Mum must have told him to leave it for now. As soon as I'd had something to eat I told Mum I wanted to go home, and we said our goodbyes.

"I didn't mean anything, Vincent," said Ewan, finally grabbing me into a bear hug.

"I know," I mumbled into his T-shirt. That made it even more annoying. My brother was brilliant at everything *and* he was mostly nice.

On the drive home Mum asked me loads of questions about *Battle Doom* – or *Battle Game* as she called it. I knew she was only asking to give me some extra attention but I answered half-heartedly. When we got home I went up to Ewan's room and settled down to play. Rather than shout up at me to come off after an hour, Mum left me to it. There was some consolation for the bad day after all.

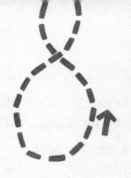

Chapter Twelve

Team Planning

The Wilderness Warriors Challenge sat heavy on my shoulders like a giant rucksack full of concrete blocks. No matter how much I wished for something to happen so that the weekend would be called off – maybe a violent hurricane in the weather forecast or for all the other teams to spontaneously cancel – nothing did, and it was suddenly Wednesday with only three days to go.

When I arrived at school I spotted Lena standing by herself in the corner of the playground. She was writing in a notebook, and she had a plastic compass on a piece of string that was looped around her neck.

"Hi," I said.

"Hi," said Lena. She took the compass from around her neck and wrapped the cord around it before putting it into her pocket.

"You have your own compass?" I said. "I'm glad someone knows what they're doing. Otherwise we could get completely lost!"

I laughed at the thought but Lena didn't break a smile.

"It's my grandpa's compass," said Lena. "Or rather, it *was* my grandpa's. Before he died."

I remembered her talking about him in form time and saying those strange things about him being an investigator and looking for vampires. It was all a bit weird and I thought I'd better change the subject. The bell went for registration and we began to walk towards the school building.

"I don't know about you, but I'm really dreading this weekend," I said.

"What are you dreading about it?" said Lena.

I was surprised that she had to ask.

"Everything really. Josh doesn't seem to be taking it very seriously, for a start. And … well, isn't it going to be a bit odd with Scarlett there? She's not very nice to you."

Lena screwed up her nose.

"I don't care about her," she said. "I just want everything to go smoothly."

"You actually *want* to go on this trip, then?" I asked.

Lena looked puzzled. "Of course I do! Why wouldn't I? I don't understand the three of you. You are all so *negative*." As we walked through the main doors she muttered, "And I don't want any of you ruining it for me."

I was about to ask what she meant when she turned to face me.

"Meet me at break time by the benches under the shade. We need to have a team talk." And with that she turned and headed to form time.

It was strange to have somewhere to go at break time. Usually, just before the bell went, I'd be busy planning what route I was going to take around the perimeter of the building, and if I had anything else to do to kill a bit more time – like hand in a form or look at the notices on the bulletin board. But today I had to meet Lena. The benches were at the top of the playground under some huge white canopies that had cost the school thousands of pounds to put up even though no one really sat there. I presumed it would be just me and Lena, so I was amazed to see Scarlett and Josh sitting with her on one of the picnic benches. I sat down opposite Lena. She had her notebook and the map from Saturday's practice session open in front of her. Under that was a plastic folder.

"Look, I don't want to be here so just say what you've got to say and let's get it over with, all right?" said Scarlett.

"Fine," said Lena. "There isn't much time left until the weekend and we still have a lot of planning to do." She seemed to have taken the role of team leader, which was probably for the best.

"I'm planning on a bit of sunbathing and sleeping," said Josh, snorting.

Lena glared at him.

"You might think this whole thing is a joke but if you aren't prepared you are going to really suffer. You do realize that, don't you?" said Lena. Josh frowned and then shrugged.

"Whatever," he said.

"What do you mean by 'suffer'?" I asked.

Lena leaned back and stretched her arms in front of her.

"If we don't plan our meals, we will be hungry. If we don't organize sharing our kit out between us, we will struggle, and if we don't all pull together and approach this as a team then there is a huge chance that we could find ourselves in serious difficulties." She sat a little taller in her seat. "Now, I know the three of you really don't want to go, but the reality is that you are not getting out of it. So the more we plan, the easier it'll be for all of us, OK?"

I'd never seen Lena like this before. She appeared so confident. I guess the power was in her hands for a change as she was the only one who seemed to know what to do.

"What have you written down there, then?" said Scarlett, grabbing Lena's notebook.

"It's a list of items for each of us to bring," said Lena. "I've shared the amounts out between us."

"You *are* joking?!" said Scarlett as she read over the pages. "I'm not carrying tinned soup! That'll weigh a ton."

I took a look over Scarlett's shoulder.

"You've got me down for a bag of rice. That's heavy too," I said. I thought of Ewan's rucksack and how I could barely lift it when it didn't even have anything in it.

"And you've only got 'snacks' under Josh's name. Why doesn't he have any heavy stuff?" said Scarlett.

"Josh will be carrying the cooking stove. And we all need to take turns to carry the tents. Is that OK, Josh?"

I expected Josh to object but he nodded. Lena ripped three pieces of paper from her notepad.

"Here are your lists. Unless, of course, any of *you* want to organize the meals?" I took my piece of paper, which had rice, crackers, fruit and porridge written on it. Scarlett stuffed her list into her pocket.

"And what about the map?" she said. "I don't get how we are supposed to know where we are going without a sat-nav or something. You'd better not get us lost and make this last any longer than it has to."

Lena folded up the map until it was in a neat little rectangular shape and she put the plastic folder on top.

"You don't need to worry about the route," she said. "You just need to turn up, bring some food, carry stuff and try to not moan too much."

I waited for Scarlett to say something but she just stood up.

"I can't believe my parents are making me do this. It's like an actual nightmare." She gave a big huff, then turned and walked off.

Josh was still hanging around like he wanted to say something.

Lena must have noticed it too. "Do you have everything you need for the trip?" she asked him. "I have another rucksack if you want to borrow it? I can bring it in tomorrow."

Josh sniffed. "Yeah, all right," he said. "Ta." He stood for a moment as if he wasn't quite sure whether to go or not, and then he headed off across the playground.

"OK. We're done," said Lena, getting up and packing her bag. I glanced at the clear plastic folder and saw that it contained what looked like old newspaper cuttings. I turned my head to read the headline of the one on the top.

HIDDEN TREASURE DEEMED AN URBAN MYTH

I was about to ask what treasure was hidden and what an 'urban myth' was when she grabbed the folder and shoved it into her bag.

"Bye, Vincent," she said. And then she walked away before I had a chance to say anything.

Chapter Thirteen

One Day to Go

On Friday lunchtime Ms Bell met us on the school field so that we could have another practice putting our tents up. I arrived at the same time as Lena.

"It looks like it's just the two of you, I'm afraid," said Ms Bell. "Scarlett and Josh clearly don't seem to realize that this weekend is a *competition*." She seemed very frustrated about that. "Anyway, you both have a go and I'll be back to check on you."

Lena took one of the tent bags and tipped it out. She pulled the ground sheet out into a square and put the tent on top.

"Do you want to start putting the poles together, Vincent?" she said.

I crouched down and picked up a pole that had miraculously turned into a long bendy pole when Mr Hearn had shown us last weekend. I fiddled with it like I knew what I was doing, and then it suddenly began to snap into place. Within a few seconds I had a long tent pole in my hand. I'd done it! Lena threaded the poles through the tent, and we managed to get it standing and pegged down just as Ms Bell arrived. She clasped her hands together in what looked like utter relief.

"Oh, well done, you two!" she said. "Maybe you've got a chance of winning after all."

I thought that was very unlikely.

After school, Mum picked me up and we went to get the last few bits I needed for the trip. Let's Go Camp! promised to have everything you might need on your outdoor adventure. All that was left on my list was a small first-aid kit, some hand sanitizer, a travel pillow and some wet wipes to keep clean.

We walked into the vast store and were faced with a display of tents, some of which looked like the size of our entire downstairs.

"I think you'll need a warm hat, Vincent. It'll get cold at night. You *will* make sure you keep warm, won't you?" said Mum.

"Yes, Mum."

She seemed a bit jittery, and I wondered if she was feeling nervous about me going. Maybe she didn't think I was cut out for it after all, just like I'd been telling her?

"Do you want to go and start looking for the other bits, Vincent?"

She went over to a row of woolly beanies that were pegged on to a washing line beside a tent. I spotted a sign that said, *First-Aid Equipment* and headed in that direction.

As I studied shelves, I noticed a man in the aisle next to me. He was wearing a grey vest that looked a bit tight around his round stomach and a pair of baggy jogging pants. He was looking at the sleeping bags and turned over one of the price labels.

"How much?" he shrieked. "You must be joking. I could buy a whole bed for that!"

Josh appeared from around a corner and walked over to him. He hadn't seen me so I put my head down and picked up a bottle of hand sanitizer and some wipes.

"I don't see why the school want you to go, Josh. It's going to cost us a fortune!" said the man. He was talking so loudly his voice was echoing around the shop.

"But the school are paying, Dad," said Josh quietly. "And Ms Bell said there was some extra money for you to get me what I need."

Josh's dad huffed. "Well, that money could be spent on useful things, not sleeping bags." I glanced over. I think it was one of the few times I'd seen Josh without a grin on his face. His dad looked at a few more prices and folded his arms.

"No. I'm not spending this sort of money. You can take your duvet from home and wrap yourself up in that," he said. "Come on."

He headed towards the exit but Josh hesitated. I thought about how Lena had offered him her rucksack earlier.

"Um, hi, Josh," I said.

He looked up, shocked to see me.

"I've got a spare sleeping bag if you want to borrow it? My dad has two. I can bring it tomorrow."

Josh gave me a small nod. "OK. Thanks," he said, and he hurried off.

We got everything that we needed, and Mum also bought me a blue beanie and some Stay Away Bug spray. Dad messaged me when I got home.

All ready for tomorrow?

I quickly typed an answer.

Nope.

He responded straight away.

You'll be fine! Remember – a life lived just out of your depth is a life fulfilled. YOU HAVE GOT THIS!!!

I groaned. Dad even texted in self-help quotations!

After dinner, Mum came to my room to help me pack, which I found incredibly overwhelming. I'm sure Mum did too. In fact, I wouldn't have been surprised if there was a Packing a Rucksack for the Wilderness Warriors Challenge Award. We wouldn't have won it, though.

We put everything I needed to take on the floor and it covered the whole carpet. We both stared at all of the stuff, and then at the rucksack.

"I'm sure we can fit it all in," said Mum. But even she looked apprehensive.

We started with clothes and waterproofs, toiletries, packets of rice, porridge and crackers, first-aid kit and then we tried to get in the sleeping bag and immediately squashed all the crackers.

"This is all so *pointless*," I said. I sat on the bed and folded my arms. Mum tipped the rucksack out to start again.

"Right. I'm going to put the sleeping bag on top of your clothes. And the packets of rice and porridge can go here in the side pockets."

She fiddled about until eventually she managed to zip the rucksack and fasten the clip.

"There! Did it," she said, smiling at me. The rucksack was so full it was standing up on its own like a small human being. I got off my bed and went to lift it up.

"It weighs a tonne!" I said. I manoeuvred it around and managed to get my arms through the thick straps, and then I stood up straight – or at least I tried to.

"How am I supposed to carry this?" I said, close to tears. "It'll be like carrying a ... a small bear on my back!"

Mum started to giggle. I couldn't believe she was finding this remotely funny. I wrestled to get the bag off and then I threw myself on to the bed. I knew I was behaving like a toddler having a tantrum, but I didn't care.

"Can I make a suggestion, Vincent?" said Mum. She didn't wait for an answer. "Try and approach the weekend with an open mind."

"You sound like Dad," I said, my voice muffled in my pillow.

"Well, he is usually right about this kind of thing. Sometimes the only one you are battling with is yourself. If you just let go of all of this … negativity, you can direct all of that energy where it's most useful. *Then* you might find you have enough strength to carry a small bear on your back."

I looked at her and she smiled down at me again.

"Trust me, Vincent. Don't overthink it." She stroked my hair. "I think you should get to sleep soon. You've got an early start tomorrow. Your dad is going to drop you off."

She gave me a kiss on the top of my head and left me to get ready for bed.

After I heard Mum turn the TV on downstairs, I went into Ewan's room. *Battle Doom* would make me feel better, and I wanted to have one more go of trying to find the diamond before the weekend was here.

I waited for the game to load and immediately

directed Fabian back to the well. Once I'd reached the bottom I could at least rule it out. As I walked up to it, the annoying travelling hawker appeared, as usual, from behind an old oak tree. He shuffled over to me, looking around in a shifty way.

"Buy my goods, young man?" he growled. "Buy my goods?"

He was carrying a tatty cloth bag which he shook at me. I tried to get around him but he kept standing right in front of me. He wasn't the sort of character that you could fight and I'd used my last sleeping potion so I was stuck. He took a lump of dirty-looking rock out from the cloth bag.

"This is a nice one for you. Hand me your coins," he rasped.

I stepped to the left, then to the right and then he grabbed hold of Fabian's arm and pulled him close, whispering into his ear, "Remember. Beauty can be found within the underestimated." His teeth were yellow like the lump in his hand and his tongue looked blackened.

I jumped as Mum suddenly poked her head around the door.

"Vincent! Come on now. You need to get to bed. Turn it off."

I hesitated for a moment, then huffed and turned off the console.

*

One of the worst feelings in the world is when you know you really need to get to sleep because you have a busy day ahead, but your brain decides to go into overdrive and just won't let you. I listened to the house creaking and the occasional car drive past. I couldn't quite believe that this time tomorrow I'd be in a tent, in the middle of nowhere, with nothing but a bit of canvas between me and the night sky. As I lay there I wished that I'd paid a bit more attention to Dad when he talked about mindfulness and relaxation. All I could remember was how he'd said something about 'returning to the breath', so I just focused my attention on my chest rising and falling.

It must have worked because I then had this weird dream where we weren't walking beside Fortune Mountain, we had to actually walk over the top of it! It was covered in snow, and Josh was wearing shorts, a Hawaiian shirt and flip-flops. Scarlett had a mobile phone in each hand, and she was talking on both of them simultaneously. Lena had the map and called out, "FOLLOW ME!" every few steps. At one point she disappeared behind a snow drift, and when I ran to catch up with her, she'd turned into a bear. She growled and lurched at me, and I jolted awake just as my alarm clock rang out.

This was it. The day I'd been dreading was here.

Today was the start of my journey to becoming a Wilderness Warrior. And I'd had about ten minutes' sleep.

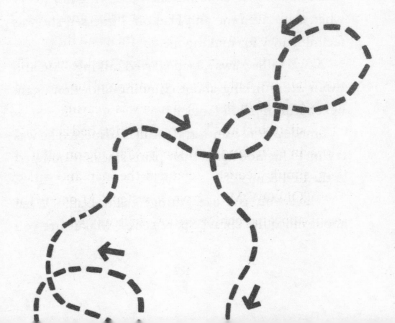

Chapter Fourteen

Ready for the Off

Mum had looked a bit like she was trying not to cry when she waved me and Dad off. I guessed she was feeling guilty for making me go.

As we pulled away, Dad started talking. "Me and Ewan are thinking about climbing Snowdon again next autumn if you fancy it?"

I made a non-committal grunt. I suspected he was trying to include me in their plans since my outburst at the barbecue.

"Have you got everything?" said Dad. "What about mosquito spray? Spare socks? Make sure you change them during the day too, won't you? You don't want to get blisters. Not that you should because, like I said, those boots of Ewan's are top-notch."

I thought about mentioning again how uncomfortable they were, but it was too late to do anything about it now.

It only took five minutes to get to school and Dad pulled up outside. I spotted Lena getting her rucksack from the boot of the car. She was dressed in her walking gear with her plastic compass around her neck. Mr Hearn must have arranged to pick Josh up as they arrived together in his little red mini. Josh was sitting in the front passenger seat, yawning.

I sat clutching the spare sleeping bag for Josh as I watched everyone head to the minibus. Ms Bell was putting the bags in the back and I could see that Scarlett was already onboard, slumped against the window.

"Come on, then, Vincent," said Dad. He got my rucksack out of the boot and swung it over his shoulder like it weighed nothing.

I stayed where I was, frozen. My limbs felt like lead. I didn't want to do this. I didn't want anyone to see how useless I was. I just wanted Dad to get back in the car and drive me home.

Dad opened the passenger door. "Shall we go?" he said. Mr Hearn walked over.

"Are we all OK over here?" he said. I clocked Dad and Mr Hearn doing 'a look' between them that adults sometimes do when they can't say anything in front of you.

"Ah, is that Josh's sleeping bag you've got there, Vincent?" said Mr Hearn through the window. "Can you go and give it to Ms Bell, please?"

I sat there for a few more seconds, wondering if I could just refuse to move, but then I spotted Dad's reflection in the wing mirror. He didn't know I could see him and his face was crumpled. He was always so happy and positive but right now he looked desperately sad. And it was all because of me.

I had to go.

I got out of the car and Mr Hearn gave me a thumbs up and headed to the minibus.

"You'll be fine," said Dad. The cheerful smile back on his face now he knew I could see him. "All you have to do is take one step at a time. OK? You've got this."

He gave me a hug then passed me my rucksack.

"Bye, Dad," I said, trying not to cry. I turned and dragged the rucksack across the car park, scraping it along the ground as I went.

Chapter Fifteen

Lena's Mysterious Grandpa

Before we got on the minibus, Ms Bell asked if anyone got travel sick and said if they did, they should sit in the front beside her. No one said anything so Mr Hearn sat there. Josh had the back seat to himself, and Scarlett was in the row in front of him on her phone, even though we had been told not to bring them. I was on the other side of the bus and Lena was in the row beside me. If the Wilderness Warriors Challenge entailed four people trying to sit as far away from each other as humanly possible on a small minibus, then we would definitely be crowned the champions.

Ms Bell and Mr Hearn were chatting excitedly at the front. It was like *they* were off on a 'life-changing adventure' and not us. We drove through our town, and Mr Hearn turned around, grinning at us.

"How about we have a sing-song?" he called. "Does anyone have any suggestions?"

Silence.

"No one fancy getting the old vocal muscles warmed up a little?"

"No!" yelled Josh from the back seat.

"I know, how about 'We Are the Champions'" to get everyone in the winning mood?" said Ms Bell. "We all know that one, don't we?"

There was still more silence, and then Ms Bell burst into song with Mr Hearn accompanying her.

"Oh, this is *so* painful," groaned Scarlett, pulling the neck of her jumper up over her head. Ms Bell and Mr Hearn managed about half of the song and then seemed to forget the lyrics so fortunately it went quiet.

I watched as the roads and buildings that I knew so well changed into areas that I had not seen before. We pulled on to a motorway and then there wasn't much else to see, apart from the occasional squashed fox or a piece of litter. The journey dragged on and on and on, and after three hours we pulled into a service station.

"I suggest you all get out and stretch your legs for a bit and have a toilet break," said Ms Bell. "We still have another two hours of travelling to go and then we'll be there. I bet the other teams will be arriving soon. Isn't it exciting?"

"How many are taking part, miss?" shouted Josh.

"There are ten teams altogether so you've only got nine others to beat," said Ms Bell.

"That'll be easy!" said Mr Hearn. And they both laughed together like this whole thing was the best fun in the world.

Lena and I slowly got up, but Scarlett pushed us out of the way to get to the front of the bus and stood tapping her fingers on the back of a seat. As soon as the doors opened she stomped down the steps and across the forecourt to the toilets. Mr Hearn, Ms Bell and Josh followed and Lena headed to the garage shop. I didn't need the toilet so I went into the shop as well.

I wandered around the aisles, looking at the crisps and sweets, and then I spotted Lena. She was peering at a stand containing maps. She twirled the stand around, chose a map with a yellow cover, then went to pay for it at the till. I thought that was a bit odd considering we already *had* a map. After she left, I went to the stand. The map with the yellow cover was much smaller than the others and the title on the front was: *Walking Routes: Fortune Mountain*. That was even stranger. I knew we were going to be close to the mountain but not actually that close. I glanced out of the window and saw that everyone was getting back on the bus so I hurried out.

"Come on, Vincent. In you get," said Mr Hearn as I climbed onboard. He was in the driver's seat this time and Ms Bell was beside him.

Scarlett had her hood pulled up covering most of her face as she slumped against the bus window. Josh seemed to be picking something off the seat next to him, and Lena was hidden behind the map she'd just bought. On the seat beside her was the map the teachers had given us. It was folded on to one section which had lines and crosses drawn on it in black pen.

Ms Bell switched the radio on as we pulled away, and I sat back and listened to the music. I thought about *Battle Doom* and how frustrating it was that I wasn't going to be able to play it for a few days.

Sometimes, when I was at school, I imagined Fabian standing exactly where I had left him, patiently waiting for my return. At this particular moment he would be by the well and the oak tree, his grey coat rippling in the breeze like it always did, as he dreamed of being allowed to return to Riverlock. I almost felt like I was letting him down in a way by not being there.

After a while I heard a rustle as Lena began to fold up her map. I remembered what Mum had said about me trying to 'go with the flow' this weekend. I sat forward and leaned over to her.

"You've worked out the route, then?" I called across the aisle. I nodded to the map that was beside her – the one with the black pen all over it. I thought she looked a bit panicked as she grabbed the map and stuffed it into a large pocket on the side of her trousers. There was a heavy-looking brown book beside her which seemed a weird thing to bring. Didn't she have enough to carry? I could make out a title along the spine: *The Life and Escapades of Walter Morgan* with a small gold embossed skull and crossbones. Lena saw me looking at the book and picked it up, along with the plastic folder she'd had at our group meeting, and tucked them both beside her.

"I hope there aren't too many hills on this walk," I said, trying to sound light-hearted and not like I was moaning.

"We can't avoid all of them," she said. I waited for her to carry on but she just stared at me. I had a tube of mints in my pocket and I offered them to her.

"Thanks," she said, taking one and popping it into her mouth. "By the way, thanks for the other day when you saved me in the canteen." She was whispering and her eyes glanced behind her to where Scarlett appeared to be sleeping.

"No problem," I said.

There was an awkward silence.

"So … um. Where did you learn how to read maps? I wouldn't have a clue."

"My grandpa taught me," said Lena.

"Oh, yes. He was the investigator," I said. "What did he do exactly?"

Lena checked behind her again and spoke in hushed tones. "Grandpa was an archivist in a big library in a city in Poland. While he was there he came across an old book written by a man who had spent fifty years investigating forgotten mysteries. Grandpa got really interested and started researching some of them himself. He wrote a blog about it, and then a man called Bernie got in touch with him after reading his blog, and they teamed up to investigate things together. But then they fell out."

"What happened?" I asked.

"Grandpa didn't like that all Bernie seemed interested in was money. He didn't care about the stories or finding out the truth. He just wanted to look for things to try and get rich."

"I see," I said.

"They once went to a remote part of Norway where there had been reports of vampires." She said it pretty matter-of-factly, as if that was quite a normal thing to do. "As soon as they got there, Bernie said that they should make up a sighting just so they could sell their story to a TV company or a newspaper and make lots of money."

"And did they find any?" I said. "Um … vampires, I mean?"

She scrunched up her nose. "No. But that doesn't mean they weren't there, of course." She began to fold her jacket into a makeshift pillow.

I laughed nervously. Not sure if she was joking or not.

"After their trip to Norway they had a big

argument and disbanded the team. Bernie just wasn't interested in the truth like Grandpa was."

It all sounded a bit childish for grown-ups to be behaving like that.

"I carried on Grandpa's blog for a while after he died. Grandpa had had a breakthrough with his research, and I wrote about how clever he was and how close he had come to solving his final investigation. I wanted everyone to know he wasn't just some eccentric old man."

I wondered what his last investigation had been. Proof of mermaids, perhaps?

"Not long after I posted the blog, Bernie emailed me telling me that he regretted how they had argued. He said he wanted to continue with Grandpa's work and could I send all the files to him. But I told him I was quite capable of carrying on myself. He was after what Grandpa had found out. I'm not silly."

"And what kind of thing have you been looking into?" I asked. "The abominable snowman, perhaps?" I grinned but she frowned at me.

Lena shook her head. "No point. We already know he exists."

I swallowed. "Really?!" I said. She raised her eyebrows and smiled, and I realized she was having me on.

Lena checked behind her again but Josh and Scarlett both had their eyes closed. They probably couldn't hear over the traffic noise anyway.

"Grandpa was looking into something really special. Something of significant value that would be a prized possession in any museum around the world. He'd got so far but had to stop when he became ill."

Her face had lit up when she'd started speaking about her grandpa, but now she looked sad.

"He was called crazy so many times for his investigating. After a while he stopped telling people what he was doing. Apart from me, that is. He used to come over each week and we'd talk for hours about his latest work. It was always so exciting! Although Mum and Dad were just like the others – they used to say it was all made-up things and that I shouldn't get so wrapped up with it."

She put her makeshift pillow against the minibus window and placed her head on it.

"But then he died. So now I don't have him to talk to and it makes me sad," she said. "I miss him very, very much."

I wasn't sure what I should say so I just said, "I'm sorry."

"Thank you," said Lena. "I'm tired so I'm going

to have a sleep now." And she abruptly turned away and closed her eyes. Lena's grandpa sounded very eccentric indeed. The fact that she was throwing herself into one of his strange investigations showed how much he meant to her, I thought. But I thought her parents were probably right and he possibly just had a wild imagination for these kinds of things.

I leaned against the window and shut my eyes as well. It would be good if I could have a bit of a sleep too, considering the amount of walking I had to get through. The gentle swaying of the bus helped me to drift off, and I must have slept for at least an hour.

I was jolted awake by Mr Hearn calling out, "Wilderness Warriors, wake up! We're here!"

I blinked and rubbed at my eyes as I looked outside. It had started to drizzle. Mr Hearn parked beside five other minibuses. There were lots of kids milling around, carrying massive rucksacks and wearing outdoor clothing. There was also a large, white gazebo which was next to a billowing sign that read: *STARTING LINE*.

Ms Bell got out of her seat and crouched down at the front of the bus.

"Before we go I just wanted to say how incredibly proud I am of you all. You are going to have the best weekend ever." Just then the rain began to pound on to the windscreen behind her. It was really hammering it down now.

"It's pouring!" said Scarlett. "I'm staying here until it stops."

Ms Bell chuckled. "If you stay on the bus you'll miss the start, won't you? Come on. Everybody off." Scarlett slumped back in her seat.

"Are you camping too, miss?" called Josh. Ms Bell looked awkward for a moment. "Um, no, Josh. I've booked a room in a lovely little bed and breakfast not far from here. But we'll be with you in spirit! Isn't that right, Mr Hearn?"

"Yes indeed!" said Mr Hearn, turning round. "And we'll be here when you finish. Is everyone ready?"

Scarlett said, "No." Josh groaned. That was about the only reaction Mr Hearn was going to manage to get out of us.

We climbed down the minibus steps and stood in the torrential rain as Mr Hearn went to the back of the bus to get our rucksacks and the tents. I pulled my hood up and stared at the starting line flag which was hanging limply in the rain.

"This is it, guys," said Scarlett. "Welcome to Hell."

Chapter Sixtee.

Are You Ready?

We lifted our rucksacks on to our backs, and the weight of mine made me feel like I was already sinking into the muddy car park. I fumbled with the clasps and managed to get one done up and I left the other one dangling. Mr Hearn had the tents.

"You are going to have to share carrying these, so who wants to go first?" he said.

Scarlett just stared at the ground so Lena took theirs. Josh was too busy watching what the other teams were doing to realize that he was being asked a question, so I reached for our tent. I tried to clip it on to the side of the rucksack but I couldn't do it. Ms Bell saw I was struggling and came over to help.

The rain was so heavy that it bounced as it hit the ground and we made our way to the gazebo and huddled together with the other nine teams. Mr Hearn went to a desk to let them know that we'd arrived. Members of the Wilderness Warriors staff, wearing grey, branded tracksuits, wandered amongst us, checking we had the right equipment and showing us where we could fill our water bottles. Josh was wearing a pair of old trainers rather than walking boots and I saw one of the team members look at them, but they must have decided that he would be OK as no one said anything to him.

Lena had the school map in a plastic wallet attached to the front of her jacket. She was looking around nervously, and I hoped she knew what she was doing. I really didn't fancy getting lost. I just wanted to get this whole thing over with and to be on the minibus heading home.

I could hear some of the other teams chatting excitedly about their estimated finish time on the first day. They even seemed thrilled about camping in torrential rain. Maybe it was because they were so bonded they were ready for anything? One team were wearing matching red rain jackets, and there was another group that had *ROYAL CRESCENT HIGH* embroidered on the front of their bright yellow woolly beanies. They didn't seem to be sagging under the weight of their rucksacks like we were, and I wondered if they'd been doing some kind of fitness training. The teacher who was with them came towards us, a look of surprise on his face when he saw Ms Bell.

"Yvonne!" he said. "Fancy seeing you here! Your school managed to scrape a few pennies together this year, then?"

He chuckled and Ms Bell instantly looked uncomfortable.

"Hello, Lionel," she said. "I see you are your usual charming self."

"Mr Mac?" said one of his students. "Can you check my water pouch? I think the tube needs readjusting."

"In a minute, Dougie," he said. He turned back to Ms Bell who had folded her arms.

"Mr Mac?" she said, raising her eyebrows. "The last I heard your name was Mr MacKenzie."

Mr Mac laughed. "Ah, Yvonne. You've never really understood teaching, have you? You need to loosen up a little bit and let them think they're on the same level as you. Then you gain their respect."

Ms Bell stood rigid, like she was a stick of dynamite about to explode. Mr Mac looked at the four of us standing beside her, and his nose scrunched up ever so slightly.

"So, this must be Team Linley High," he said, taking us all in. He turned to Ms Bell. "And you're seriously hoping to win with *that* rabble?"

"Why not?" said Ms Bell. "They've got just as much chance as your team."

Mr Mac seemed to find that hilarious and he shook his head.

"Still delusional, I see, Yvonne," he said. "Well, let the best team win, eh?"

Ms Bell opened her mouth to say something, but he had already headed back to his group.

"Who was *that* idiot?" said Scarlett.

"*That* idiot was my ex-husband," said Ms Bell. "We met when we studied chemistry together at university. Fortunately, I don't have anything to do with him any more."

Mr Hearn appeared and I noticed Ms Bell seemed to relax a little.

"Not long now, team!" he said. "They're getting ready to start."

After a few minutes of standing around, a woman stepped up on to a wooden plinth. She was also wearing a grey tracksuit with the Wilderness Warriors logo on the chest and her black hair was woven into plaits, which were bunched back in a low ponytail.

"Hi, everyone! Can I have your attention, please?" she called out. There was a general hushing sound and everyone went silent.

"Thank you for joining us today. I'm sorry we couldn't arrange better weather for you!" she said. Everyone laughed, apart from us. "My name is Carmen and I am the team manager for this Wilderness Warriors Challenge. I just wanted to say that I hope you have a thrilling, exhilarating and exciting trek. I have complete and utter faith in you all and I know you can do this. Can you DO THIS?"

A lot of teams shouted back with a very enthusiastic "YEAH!" and I spotted a few air punches. All we managed was a snort from Josh.

"That's amazing! I can see some great warriors out there already," said Carmen, smiling. "I'm now going to pass you over to my colleague, Dale, who is going to explain how you'll be starting off. Good luck, everyone!"

Carmen got down off the plinth and a tall, muscular man with sandy-brown hair and bright blue eyes jumped up in one bound. He had a clipboard tucked under a large bicep, and his face broke into a dazzling white-toothed grin.

"Hi, everyone! My name is Dale and a big welcome to the Wilderness Warriors Challenge. How are you all doing?"

There was a general 'Whoop!' from the crowd.

"Yeah, that's great! So much energy!" said Dale. "Well, you are going to need it, for sure. Right, we are going to do a staggered start as we don't want you to just follow each other around now, do we?"

He laughed, as did the rest of the staff and a few of the teachers.

"There will be three checkpoints along the walk today where you can refill your water and ask us any questions. The first checkpoint should be a few hours into your walk if you have planned your route well. We will regroup this evening at the campsite, then we'll do another staggered start tomorrow."

I hoped that there would be some toilets at the campsite. I wasn't planning on just going behind a bush or anything.

Dale carried on. "As a team you will have decided

what route is best for your group, factoring in your individual strengths and weaknesses." I looked at Lena. Had she done this when she'd been planning ours? I wanted to catch her eye to find out, but she was staring at Dale.

"One little tip that I can give you is that if you find yourself heading directly towards Fortune Mountain then you are definitely going the wrong way! You need to go around it, OK?" Everyone seemed to find that notion absolutely hilarious.

"We are going to call you to the starting line one team at a time, and I want the rest of you to stay here. And this is your last chance to use the facilities so do make use of them if you need to go! Can we have Team Barrington Academy first, please."

A girl in a group let out a squeal and she and her three teammates followed Dale to the start. They didn't seem to have any matching clothes like the others, but they started chanting "TEAM B.A., TEAM B.A., TEAM B.A." as they walked.

The four of us huddled closer together, mainly because the rain was now being blown sideways underneath the gazebo rather than for any last-minute bonding. There was the sound of a whistle and the first group set off. I watched as they headed across the start line and veered to the right and behind some trees.

"All right, team?" said Ms Bell. "Do you have any questions before you head off?"

I had a million. How did I put a tent up again? What should I do if I saw a snake? How do you go to the toilet behind a tree and what if it wasn't just a wee?

But none of us said anything.

"Right. Those of you who have them with you, it's time to hand over your mobile phones. We'll look after them until the end of the trip," said Mr Hearn.

Mine was at home and I knew that Josh didn't have one at all, but Lena handed hers over.

"Scarlett?" said Mr Hearn. "I saw you using yours on the bus. Can we have it, please?"

Scarlett rolled her eyes and passed her phone to Ms Bell. Mr Hearn then took a plastic wallet out of the inside pocket of his jacket.

"This is your emergency phone. It's in a sealed wallet. If a situation arises where you need to call us, just break the tag to open the zip. My number, Ms Bell's number and the numbers of the Wilderness Warriors team are already saved on the phone. But obviously if the situation calls for it, dial 999."

I wished he hadn't made it sound quite so dramatic. I was nervous enough as it was.

"Vincent, you can look after this. I suggest you put it in the bottom of your rucksack as you almost certainly won't be needing it. Remember, if at the end of the challenge we find that the tag is broken and there isn't a reasonable explanation why, you will be disqualified."

He passed the sealed wallet to me, and I unzipped the top of my bag and stuffed it down the side. I had a sudden thought.

"What if anyone needs us?" I said. "I mean, say there's an emergency at home and we need to get back. How will you contact us?"

Ms Bell smiled kindly.

"I'm sure that won't happen, Vincent," she said. "But you'll never be more than a few hours away from a checkpoint. Your parents have our mobile numbers so they would call us and we'd get a message to the organizers who will see you on your route."

Mr Hearn and Ms Bell started talking about something and I felt an elbow in my back.

"Worried Mummy is going to miss you too much, are you, Vincey baby?"

"Shut up, Scarlett," I muttered. She grinned and raised her hands as if she was scared of me.

It took ages for everyone to set off as there was

a long gap between each team, but eventually there were just two teams left. Us and Royal Crescent High.

Dale returned from the starting line with his clipboard. "OK, Team Linley High, follow me, please!"

It was us. Ms Bell and Mr Hearn both looked a bit like they might cry, and they patted each of us on the back.

"You can do it; just believe in yourselves," said Ms Bell.

"We'll see you at the end!" said Mr Hearn.

We stepped out into the pouring rain and followed Dale to the start line where we stood in a row. My rucksack was already digging into my shoulders. I tried to readjust it a little but it didn't feel any better. Dale looked at the soaking clipboard and then checked his watch.

"Are you ready, guys?" he said, rain running down his face. Lena nodded and gave a thumbs up and I hoped that would be enough for him, but he didn't seem to be very happy.

"I said, are you ready, guys?" he said, louder this time and with a big grin on his face.

"Yes," we said reluctantly in unison.

"Come on, just hurry up," mumbled Scarlett.

"On your marks, get set, go!" said Dale, blowing on his whistle.

We trundled across the line and that was it.

The Wilderness Warriors Challenge had begun.

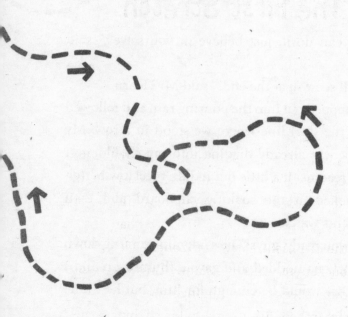

Chapter Seventeen

The First Stretch

The walk took us on a pathway that led through a small woodland. We were quite sheltered from the weather to start with, but then the trees thinned out and we headed into the open. The wind had picked up and the rain lashed at us horizontally. It was like having buckets of water constantly thrown in your face, and my cheeks were stinging.

Lena marched on ahead, followed by me and Scarlett with Josh behind us.

It took precisely twenty minutes before Scarlett started moaning.

"My rucksack is *well* heavy. I'm sure I'm carrying more than anyone else. Oi! Lena! Stop! You're not carrying enough!"

Lena either didn't hear or pretended that she hadn't, and her bottle-green rucksack and navy-blue jacket hood carried on moving away.

"Lena's got the tent as well as her own stuff, Scarlett," I said. "You're going to be carrying that too soon."

Scarlett wiped the rain out of her face. She must have been wearing make-up as she had black smears under her eyes; her fringe was plastered to her forehead.

"No way am I carrying *anything* else," she said. I didn't envy Lena. Josh was a bit of an idiot but I didn't think he'd actually refuse to carry the tent when it was his turn.

"How far are we going to walk before we actually have a break?" said Scarlett. "Hey, Lena! When are we going to stop?"

Lena carried on walking. Scarlett then began to get angry with nature.

"I don't see the point of grass. I mean, what actually is up with it? And why don't they just flatten all the hills so that we don't have to go up and down them? Hills are *the worst*."

"We haven't been up a hill yet," I said. Scarlett looked back at where we'd just come from which was a slight incline and definitely not a hill.

"Urgh. This is just SO POINTLESS!" she yelled. The yell made Lena briefly glance at us before carrying on.

My left foot was rubbing against the back of my boot, and I was sure I was going to end up with a big blister.

"Why is she walking so fast, anyway?" said Scarlett. "It's not like we are actually going to win this thing."

She was right about Lena walking quickly. She seemed to have a good technique where she leaned forward slightly with her head down and her arms swinging beside her. I wondered if walking like that made it easier to carry a heavy rucksack so I tried it myself, but it just meant I couldn't really see where I was going.

Lena stopped for a moment to study the map and check her compass. We caught her up but she set off again.

I looked back at Josh who had his thumbs under each of his straps as he lolloped along. He seemed to be in a world of his own.

"When *is* this rain ever going to stop?" Scarlett said out loud for about the tenth time. I had rainwater running down my cheeks, and it was now finding its way down my neck and on to my back and chest. I knew that I couldn't get wet beneath my coat or my clothes would start to rub against my skin and make it sore. And I had enough of that with my painful boot.

"Can we stop, please?" I shouted. Scarlett halted immediately and wriggled out of her rucksack.

"LENA!" she bellowed. Lena turned around and walked back to join us.

"What are you stopping for?" she said. "We've got to keep going!"

Scarlett took her water bottle out of her bag and had a swig.

"It's Vincent's fault," she said. "He's finding it really, really tough."

I was astounded. "What? No, I'm not!" I said. "I just need to adjust my coat. I'm getting wet."

"Really?" said Scarlett. "I'm not sure if you've noticed but we are ALL getting wet."

That wasn't what I meant! I just wanted to stop the water from going *inside* my coat. That was all. And I wanted to try tightening up my left boot to see if that might help with the rubbing.

"Well, don't take too long," said Lena. She looked around and then studied the map again. Everything looked the same to me: a thick, grey sky and soggy, green fields.

I took off my rucksack and adjusted my collar, pulling it up a bit higher. Then I undid the clips on my boots, wiggled my foot, and clipped them back again. Dad had put them on for me and they were much easier than the laces.

Josh finally caught us up.

"What's the big hurry?" he said to Lena. "Are you trying to win or something?" He laughed. Even the pouring rain didn't seem to dampen his humour.

Lena wiped some of the rainwater off the map.

"I just think we should stay on a tight schedule so that we can have a decent rest later, that's all," she said. "And the sky looks a bit brighter where we're heading so it'll hopefully be dry."

I looked to where she had nodded. The sky in that direction was a light grey rather than dark grey so maybe she was right.

"I reckon we'll be at the first checkpoint in about two hours," said Lena. "Come on. Let's go."

She walked off again and I lifted my rucksack on to my back.

"Urgh. This is torture," said Scarlett. "I can't see why anyone would want to do this kind of thing for pleasure. They must be, like, weirdos or something. Can you imagine choosing to do this?"

I thought of the many walks that Dad and Ewan had done together and didn't say anything. It might not be something I was keen on but they definitely weren't weirdos. Lena was right about the rain, though, and after half an hour or so it began to ease off. I took my hood down.

Scarlett had been quiet for a while but then she started up again.

"I still don't remember you at all, you know," she said. "Who do you usually sit with in form time?"

I took a step to one side, avoiding a large rock on the ground. "No one. I sit in the corner at the back," I said quietly. Scarlett screwed her nose up as she thought about it. "So who do you hang out with then? Maybe I know them."

"Whoever is around really," I said, trying to sound vague. Scarlett frowned and I was worried she was going to start grilling me further, so I thought I'd fire a question back at her.

"You're friends with Melanie and Holly, aren't you?"

"Yeah. I wish they were here too. At least it'd be bearable, then. They're my best mates."

We carried on in silence for a few paces.

"And why are they your best friends?" I asked.

Scarlett frowned. "What do you mean?" she said.

"It's just that ... well, I see the three of you arguing a lot and then you make up, and then you argue again. And ... well, I just wondered why you are such good friends with them if you don't really get on that well."

Scarlett stared at the ground as we walked, but she didn't say anything as she kicked at a stone.

"Better to have friends than be a billy-no-mates like *you*," she said finally. "That's *well* sad."

I felt my face flush and I glanced over at her.

"I think I'd rather be on my own than have friends who were horrible to each other," I blurted out.

I couldn't believe I'd answered back! My heart pounded as I waited for her to start shouting at me and calling me names or worse. But she didn't. Maybe it was tiredness or the fact that there was no audience to hear her, but she kept a fixed scowl on her face and we walked for the next hour and a half in complete silence.

Before long I realized that we were heading

towards our first proper hill. It didn't look too bad, but I knew it would be hard work with the weight we were all carrying on our backs.

"Can we stop? I need a wee!" shouted Josh. Lena came to a halt and Scarlett and I joined her while Josh rushed off behind a bush.

"We really need to pick up the pace," said Lena sternly. "Look. We've already been caught up."

Coming around a bend and heading towards us were Team Royal Crescent High wearing their yellow woolly beanies – the team with Ms Bell's ex-husband as their teacher. With every other step, one of the team made a 'Hur-rup' sound. The three of us stared at them as they strode our way.

"They look so professional," I said. They were also a team of two boys and two girls but they were walking much faster than us. The boy at the front started singing some kind of military motivational call the three behind sang back.

"We are gonna be the best!"
"We are gonna be the best!"
"We ain't gonna have no rest!"
"We ain't gonna have no rest!"

"Urgh. What is wrong with them?" sniped Scarlett.

When they got closer, the leader spotted us and the four of them circled around us. They each had a plastic tube snaking out the top of their rucksacks and over their shoulder, and all four of them began to suck on the end. I realized that they were drinking pouches of water stored in their rucksacks. They'd didn't even need to stop to take their bottles out of their bags.

"Is there a problem, Team Linley?" said the boy who had been calling out the chants. "You are looking a little ... bewildered."

"Everything's fine," said Lena, holding herself a little taller. The boy took a few more sips from the tube, before clipping it back on to his strap.

"Are you sure?" he said. "I mean, we weren't expecting to catch anybody up. Mr Mac says we are fast but ... wow, you guys must be *slow*!" The rest of his team laughed.

"Hang on, though, Dougie," said one of the girls to him. "Maybe one of them has an injury." She looked back at us. "Do any of you have an injury?"

"Actually, where *is* your other teammate?" said Dougie. "The tall kid. Looks a bit ... gormless."

They began to look around.

"He's ... um ... going to the toilet," I said.

Just then, Josh appeared from behind the bush, dragging his rucksack beside him.

"All right?" he said, nodding at the group and dumping his bag on the ground.

Team Royal Crescent High looked Josh up and down, and Dougie stared at his feet.

"Oh. Are those minimalist hiking shoes?" he said.

Josh looked at his feet.

"You what?" he said. The trainers were completely brown from the mud, and he tried to scrape some of it off on to the grass.

"Are they minimalist shoes?" said Dougie. "You know, the ones with a zero drop? Mr Mac has a pair and he said they are brilliant for walking. How are you finding them?"

Josh grinned. "I dunno what you're talking about, mate," he said. "These are my dad's old trainers, aren't they?"

The boy flinched as if someone had clicked their fingers right in front of his face. "Oh. I see," he said. The other boy in their team snorted and they all seemed to be trying not to laugh.

"We'd better be off now. Our plan is to win this thing," said Dougie. "Good luck, Team Linley! I think you're going to need it!"

He laughed and the rest of the team laughed in response. I thought it must be like travelling with your own personal echo. Team Royal Crescent High marched off, and we watched as they trotted nimbly up the hill and disappeared over the peak.

"Idiots," mumbled Scarlett.

"Right. Let's get going," said Lena. "Come on."

We reluctantly followed her up the hill as she shouted advice over her shoulder.

"Try to keep your weight distribution equal as you walk. Don't look up. Just focus on the ground in front of you and keep walking!"

Scarlett seemed to actually listen to Lena this time, and she put her head down and marched on. My foot was really hurting so I slowed my pace and before long I was walking next to Josh.

"You OK?" I asked.

"Yeah," he said. I looked at his trainers, which were like two lumps of mud at the end of his legs. They couldn't have much grip to them at all.

I didn't know anything about Josh apart from the fact that he was always getting in trouble for doing silly things. Only a few weeks ago he'd been put in detention for chucking his school books on to the school building roof for 'a laugh'.

"It's a lot of walking, isn't it?" I said, smiling. Josh nodded. I guessed he didn't know what to say to me either.

"Do you like gaming?" I asked.

Josh screwed up his nose and shook his head. "Nah," he said. "Those things are *well* boring. You don't play, do you?"

I swallowed.

"Um. A bit," I said.

Josh started laughing. "Oh, what? Are you like one of those saddos who never leaves their room and just sits with headphones on talking to a computer or something?"

I wish I'd never said anything now. I *was* one of those saddos.

"I only play now and then," I lied. "Actually, some people think playing on computer games turns you into a zombie or something, when in fact—"

Josh let out a huge, pretend yawn.

"Oh, sorry?" he joked. "What was that you were saying? It was *so* interesting."

I didn't get Josh. He seemed to always feel like he had to joke about something.

I decided not to try to explain and just kept walking. After a while Josh stopped and stared across at something on the side of the hill. I looked to where he was staring but couldn't see anything.

"What is it?" I asked.

"I thought I saw … a bird. But it was just a leaf."

He carried on walking, and I made the mistake of looking up and seeing how far we still had to go. Lena and Scarlett were getting further and further away.

"What sort of bird did you think it was?" I asked.

"A stonechat," he said. "I've not seen one before."

"Are you a … birdwatcher?" I said.

"So what?" said Josh. He looked a bit flushed.

"And you know about them, then?" I asked. "What the different species look like?"

"Yeah. Kind of," said Josh. "My nan gave me a book on wildlife for my eighth birthday. I remember all the names and what they look like and stuff."

I wasn't expecting this *at all*.

"Where do you go birdwatching?" I asked.

"I don't," he said. "I haven't got any binoculars or anything. You need them to be a proper spotter. My nan gave me a pair but Dad sold them to a bloke in the pub."

"That's horrible," I said.

"He needed the money, didn't he?" snapped Josh.

"Anyway, it's only birds. No one cares about them, do they?"

He stomped onwards up the hill and I realized that this was the first time I'd seen Josh not making a joke or laughing about something that wasn't funny. It was also pretty clear that he was a bit sensitive about his family.

I was now at the back of the group. I put my head down and stared at the ground again and kept walking. My thighs burned and the back of my heel felt like it had broken glass rubbing against it.

When I looked up it was just a few steps to the peak of the hill. I stood by Lena, Scarlett and Josh as they peered down the other side.

"We're nearly there," said Lena.

At the bottom of the hill I could see a couple of figures standing beside a Wilderness Warriors flag and a white, plastic table.

We had made it to the first checkpoint.

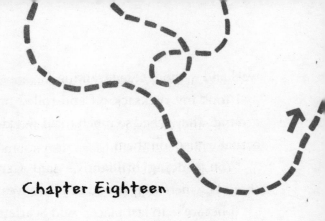

Chapter Eighteen

Checkpoint Number One

Wilderness Warrior leaders, Dale and Carmen, were standing by a folding plastic table that was laden with jugs of water, fruit and energy bars.

"You're here at last," bellowed Dale as he stood with his hands on his hips. "Come and refill your bottles and grab yourselves a snack. How are you all doing?"

Scarlett sank to the ground.

"It's so HARD," said Scarlett. "There's so much *walking*."

Dale grinned. "Yep. It wouldn't be a Warriors

weekend without some walking."

I took my rucksack off and rolled my shoulders around. They ached so much that I wondered if I had actual bruises on them.

"You're doing brilliantly," said Carmen. "You should be incredibly proud of yourselves."

"I bet we're in last place," said Scarlett. "I vote we just give up. Who's with me?"

Josh raised his hand. "Me!" he said. Scarlett looked at me next, but before I could say anything, Carmen stepped in.

"Let's not be too hasty, shall we?" she said. "Starting is the hardest part sometimes. It can be a shock to your body when you realize how tough these few days are going to be. But look at you all! You're still here!"

"That's only because we *can't* leave," said Josh. "Show me the nearest bus stop and I'm out of here."

Carmen laughed. "Ah, you're not fooling me," she said. "I think you are actually surprising yourself at how well you're doing."

Josh shrugged. I kind of knew what Carmen was getting at. It was a miracle that we hadn't given up. And even though we weren't exactly friends, we hadn't fallen out with each other just yet, and we were still walking as a team.

Josh lay on his back and put his head on his rucksack.

"If we're not quitting, can we just stay here, then?" he said. "It's actually quite comfy."

He wriggled as if he was settling down for a sleep and pretended to snore. Me and Scarlett laughed and his eyes sprang open, possibly surprised that someone found him funny for once. I looked over at Lena to see if she was laughing as well, but she was staring down at something in her lap. It was the map she'd bought at the motorway services. Beside her was the clear plastic folder that she'd had on the bus. She opened the folder and took out some papers, but a breeze caught a couple and they fluttered away across the grass.

"I'll grab those for you," said Dale. He trotted after the papers and picked them up, glancing at them before handing them over to Lena.

"Been doing a bit of local research, have you?" he asked.

"No. Not really," she said. She quickly stuffed the papers back into the folder as Dale watched her.

"Would you like me to check your route before you head off?" said Dale. He twisted his head to take a look at Lena's map, but she folded it away.

"No, thank you," she said. "I'm fine."

"You're heading towards some breathtaking scenery, aren't they, Dale?" said Carmen.

Dale nodded. "Oh, yes. It's stunning. But I'm afraid you'd better get moving again before your legs get too stiff. At least the rain has stopped."

We slowly got to our feet and I lifted my rucksack on to my back. It felt heavier than it had before.

"We need to swap who's carrying the tents now," said Lena. "We can change over at the next checkpoint." She held the tent out to Scarlett, who looked at Dale and Carmen before taking it. Josh took ours and clipped it on to the bottom of his rucksack.

"Good luck, guys," said Dale. "We'll see you at the next checkpoint. And, remember, I can always look at your route plan at the next stage if you need. You just have to ask." He directed that comment at Lena, but she was looking into the distance and then back at her map, presumably working out which way to go. I was a bit worried that she was struggling. The last thing we needed right now was to get lost.

We followed Lena along another pathway which meandered through a valley of thick green grass.

As soon as we were out of Carmen and Dale's sight, Scarlett thrust the tent into Lena's stomach.

"If you think I'm carrying this, you've got another think coming," she said.

Lena grabbed it before it fell to the ground. "But it's your turn, Scarlett!" she said.

"*But it's your turn, Scarlett!*" said Scarlett in a whiny voice that was nothing like Lena's. "Oh, grow up, Lena."

Lena looked at me and I shrugged. I felt bad for her but I didn't know how to make Scarlett carry it. Lena huffed and clipped the tent on to her bag.

We trudged on. It might not have been raining but the muddy ground was tricky and I skidded a few times. Walking on slippery surfaces wasn't something I was very good at. When I stumbled for about the fifth time, Josh began to laugh.

"You're going to stack it in a bit!" he said. I knew he didn't mean anything by it but I was beginning to feel really angry. It was all right for him. He could walk OK even wearing those ridiculous trainers. After a few paces my foot slid out at an angle and I fell on to my back, my rucksack cushioning the fall.

Josh clapped his hands together.

"Oh, that was so funny!" he said. "You're like a

baby deer or something!"

Lena must have heard the commotion because she turned around.

"Are you OK, Vincent?" she yelled.

I didn't answer as I was concentrating on trying to get to my feet again. It was hard with the weight of the rucksack pulling me backwards, but I managed to get on to my knees. I went to stand but toppled forward, falling flat on my face in the mud.

"Urgh!" said Scarlett. "You look like you've been rolling in poo." Josh was still laughing like some deranged hyena.

I felt Lena grab the back of my rucksack, and she pulled as I clambered up again.

"Just leave him alone," she said. "He has dyspraxia, if you must know!"

"He's got what?" said Scarlett, taking a step backwards like I had an infectious disease or something.

I had no idea how Lena knew. I frowned at her.

"Your brother mentioned it to my brother at college," she said. "It's no big deal."

"I know. And I can look after myself," I snapped. Although, saying that, I still had to hold on to Lena's arm to get upright. I tried to wipe some of the mud off my face but I felt it smear across my cheeks. I wanted to cry. I was cold, I was soaked, every muscle ached, my foot throbbed and now I was utterly humiliated. I just wanted to go home.

"Yes. Let's just keep moving and get this over with," I said.

Lena walked off to join Scarlett and I fell into step with Josh. After we walked for a few minutes in silence he began to talk.

"What's that dyspraxia thing you've got, then?" he asked. "Is it painful?"

"It's nothing like that. It's a condition that means I find it hard to do things that involve a lot of coordination or balance. Like walking on muddy ground," I said. "Or being organized. School can be a bit of a nightmare."

Josh didn't say anything and I waited for him to crack some sort of joke, but he didn't.

"I remember now, you forget to bring your stuff in a lot, don't you?" he said. "Even I'm not that bad! I thought you were just really lazy or something."

I sighed. "Yeah, that's what a lot of people think. If you've got dyspraxia then sometimes people think you're just ... I don't know, dim or something. And that you're *deliberately* late or disorganized. But it's not like that at all. I find things hard that other people do easily."

I took a breath. That was the most I'd said to anyone about my condition *ever*.

"But you can play computer games?" said Josh. "That must need some kind of coordination, doesn't it?"

"Yeah. I found it hard at first. It depends on what game I play. But I'm really good at it now."

Josh nodded. "Cool," he said.

And that was it. I was expecting a few more questions and possibly some wisecracks, but he didn't seem to want to know anything else.

We got to checkpoint number two and met Carmen again with another team member called Phoebe. We took our rucksacks off but didn't sit down this time and just had something to eat before carrying on. This section was mostly flat grassland and we walked in silence as we rapidly ran out of energy. My back was aching, my blister was feeling raw and I had mud caked all down my trousers. Checkpoint number three appeared thankfully quickly and Dale was waiting this time with his jeep parked up with the boot open, full of refreshments.

"You're doing so well!" said Dale. "You'll be pleased to hear that this is the last section of the day, and it should be a much shorter walk. You'll be at the campsite before you know it!"

"Hoo-ray," said Scarlett. "I can't believe I actually *want* to sleep in a tent right now."

None of us took our rucksacks off for this break as we realized how much heavier they felt when you had to put them back on. We had some juice but we all just wanted to get day one over with.

"Let's get going," said Lena. "Like Dale said, it's not far now."

We carried on across a field and then the terrain changed as we headed on to moorland. I was surprised how colourful everything was. On either side of the path were clumps of bright purple heather, and we were soon surrounded by small hills in different shades of green, yellow and brown. It was getting darker and we passed some orange-coloured bracken that seemed to almost glow in the dim light. I imagined all the other teams were now relaxing, wiggling their toes in the fresh air as they took off their damp socks and heavy boots. I was fighting an urge to just stop and sit on the ground but when we got to the peak of a low hill, Lena let out a gasp.

"Look! There it is!" she called. "There's Fortune Mountain!"

We gathered around her. Beyond the small hills, and shrouded in a grey hazy mist, was the silhouette of a great mountain. It loomed like a giant ship sailing along the horizon. There wasn't any snow at the top like there had been on Ms Bell's assembly slide, but there was a dark sky behind it which made it look even more dramatic.

"Isn't it incredible?" said Lena. Her eyes were sparkling and she had a big smile on her face.

"It does look pretty cool," said Scarlett. Which was the first positive thing I'd heard her say.

"I'm just glad we haven't got to go up it," said Josh.

"Come on," said Lena. "There's still a way to go."

We trudged on, and every time I looked up, the mountain edged a tiny bit closer. After what felt like miles and miles we were nearly there.

I stopped. "Look! There's the camp!" I shouted.

Tucked on the side of a small valley was a scattering of tents. I could make out a few of the other teams sitting and eating dinner and my stomach grumbled in hunger.

"At last," said Scarlett. "This has been the longest day *ever*."

We set off again and even managed to speed up a little now that we knew we were close to finishing the first day.

"I'm starving," said Scarlett.

"Me too," I said.

"And me!" said Lena.

"I'm so famished I could eat my own socks!" said Josh. For the first time that day I noticed that we all had smiles on our faces. They were only small smiles, but knowing that we had nearly completed day one cheered us all up a little.

But our smiles were short-lived because as soon as we entered the campsite, everyone began to laugh.

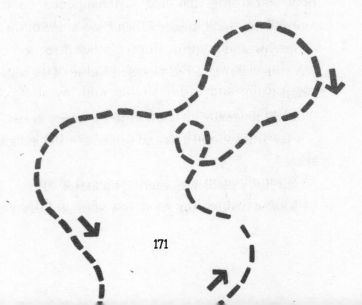

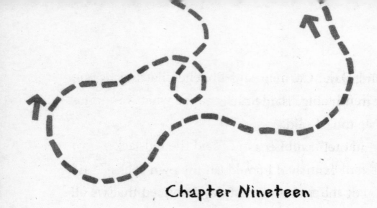

Chapter Nineteen

Our First Camp

At first, I thought they might have been laughing about something that had just happened on the campsite that we'd missed. Then I saw some of them whispering and pointing fingers in our direction.

A boy wearing a red jacket stood up and began to clap.

"And they made it! Team Linley are here at last!"

A few others joined in and someone whistled and cheered.

I felt like a gladiator entering an arena.

I looked around for some of the organizers and

spotted Dale, Carmen and Phoebe chatting by the water refill table. They didn't realize what was going on.

"What took you so long?" said the red-jacket boy. "We've all been here for *hours*!"

"Look at him!" said a girl, pointing to me. "OMG. He must have face-planted!"

I wiped at the mud on my cheeks.

"Do you think they got lost?" muttered someone beside the girl. I noticed some of the other teams weren't joining in and looked away. But the majority were laughing.

"Why are they being so horrible?" said Scarlett. She looked shocked to be on the receiving end of the nasty comments.

The boy called Dougie from Team Royal Crescent High, who we'd met near the hill, jumped up and began to walk beside Josh. "How are your dad's trainers holding up?" He pointed to Josh's feet and gasped. "Oh no! They've turned into lumps of mud!"

I waited for Josh to reply with some wisecrack or laughter, but he seemed lost for words. And then the most surprising thing of the day happened. Scarlett stood in front of Dougie and glared at him.

"I think you should bog off and go back to your

other yellow-beanie-wearing minions, don't you?" she snapped.

Dougie raised his eyebrows and laughed in her face.

"You four are *so* useless," he said. Then he turned to his friends. "Give it up for Team Useless, everyone!"

All four of them clapped and a few others joined in, and then Dougie sat down, picking up a bowl of steaming food. Their fun was over. For now, at least.

"Come on," said Lena. "Let's go and set up over there."

We followed Lena and got to work putting up our tents. Josh tried to help this time, but I couldn't remember what to do and I couldn't get the poles to fit together like I had when I practised with Lena. An hour later, and with everyone else watching and sniggering into their hot cocoa, we still hadn't got our camp ready. Even Lena was struggling. Dale and Carmen came over and said they couldn't actually help us as it was against the rules of the challenge, but they could offer advice. Eventually, with their instructions and Josh doing most of the fiddly bits for us, we ended up with two upright tents, although ours was sagging a bit in the middle.

"And they did it at last!" shouted Dougie. "Let's hear it again for Team Useless!"

"Oh, just shut up!" yelled Scarlett back, making Josh laugh.

Dale went over to the group, probably to tell them to lay off.

"I hate this," said Scarlett, going red with anger. "If being here wasn't bad enough, we've got to put up with everyone being horrible as well! How can they be so mean?"

Lena raised her eyebrows at me. It was quite unbelievable that Scarlett didn't realize how mean *she* could be herself.

There wasn't a toilet block as I'd hoped, so I wandered off to find a bush that I could hide behind. On the way back I walked past a tent with a group who I remembered were the first to set off – Team Barrington Academy. Two girls were talking and they didn't see or hear me coming. I caught the tail end of their conversation.

"… I can't see them finishing it, can you? They're *so* unprepared."

"I know. Did you see that boy's shoes? He doesn't even have walking boots! That loud girl won't last long either. She's all mouth."

One of the girls elbowed the other one when she spotted me walking by their guy ropes. I kept my head up and pretended I hadn't heard anything.

When I got to our tent, I unclipped my boots and took them off. On the back of my left heel I had a large, yellow-looking blister. I prodded it with my finger and it stung. I changed into a clean pair of socks, remembering what Dad had told me about how important it was to put fresh ones on now and then.

Lena lit the camp stove and warmed up some tomato soup. Scarlett was sitting by her tent with her arms around her knees. She looked sad and I guessed the others teasing us had upset her.

I rummaged in the depths of my bag for the crackers that I'd packed with Mum. That felt like weeks ago now. The crackers were broken into bits, but I shared out some fragments, and it wasn't long before we were sitting with bowls of warm soup in our hands.

"This tastes so nice," said Josh. "Thanks, Lena." He had a smear of orange on the top of his lip.

"No problem," said Lena. "Are you all right? You know ... after the others said stuff about your shoes."

Josh shrugged. "Yeah. It don't bother me what people think." He laughed again, but this time his smile didn't seem as genuine.

"I guess they're right, though," said Scarlett. "We are useless. We are *never* going to finish this thing. I vote we just quit and go home."

"What?" said Lena. "But we can't!"

"It *is* a bit of a nightmare," said Josh.

Lena looked over at me with panic on her face. I shook my head. "I'm sorry, Lena, but Scarlett's right. We're just not cut out for this. All the other teams are prepared and like professional hikers or something! Can you really see us managing two more days?"

Lena looked devastated.

"Where's that phone, Vincent?" said Scarlett. "Let's call Ms Bell and Mr Hearn and tell them to come and get us."

She reached for my rucksack and plunged her hand inside.

"No! Stop it, Scarlett!" said Lena. "You haven't thought this through! There is … there is so much more to this trip!"

Josh snorted. "If you're going to say that we are going to win it then don't bother!"

Scarlett pulled the plastic wallet with the phone inside out of my bag. She put her hand on the tag to snap it open when Lena dived forward and snatched it.

"Hey, Lena!" Scarlett yelled.

Everyone in the camp looked over to see what was going on. Lena held the phone behind her back.

"Just wait a minute, OK?" she said. Her eyes were blinking and it was like she was trying to get something straight in her head.

Scarlett began to slip her boots on.

"Actually, we don't need the phone," she said. "I'll just go and tell Dale and Carmen myself."

Lena grabbed her arm.

"Hang on! There's … there's something I need to tell you."

Scarlett huffed. "What?" she snapped.

Lena glanced around at the other teams and then she kneeled down in front of us. She beckoned for Scarlett to sit too and the four of us were in a tight huddle.

"What if I told you there was something we could do that was better than winning?" she said in hushed tones.

Josh scratched his chin. "What do you mean?"

Lena paused for a second, then took a deep breath.

"What if there was a different challenge that we could do? Something that would make completing the Wilderness Warriors Challenge look like … child's play."

Lena's eyes looked bright and excited in the glow

of the nearby campfire.

"A different challenge?" I said. "What kind of different challenge?"

"What are you talking about?" said Scarlett.

Lena checked behind her to make sure no one was listening. And then she turned to us with a smile on her face.

"How do you fancy finding some treasure?" she whispered.

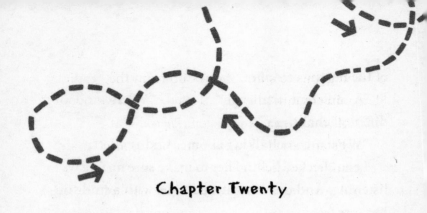

Chapter Twenty

Lena's Great Plan

"Treasure?" screeched Scarlett. "What do you mean, *treasure*?"

Lena waved her hand and shushed her, checking to see if anyone around us had heard. A few heads in the other teams perked up and stared at us.

"Keep your voice down, Scarlett!" she said. "I have some highly confidential information on the whereabouts of a valuable item not far from here. And we don't want anyone to hear, OK?"

"Oh, come on, we're not primary school kids, Lena," said Scarlett. "You're clearly making it up to try and get us to stay." She got up from the ground. "I'm going to talk to Dale."

"No!" said Lena. "Just listen. *Please?*"

"Let's at least hear what Lena has to say," I said. Lena smiled at me.

"Yo! Are Team Useless having a bust-up?" called Dougie from the other side of the bonfire. "Ready to quit already, are you?"

Scarlett stuck out her tongue at him and Lena got up.

"I'm going to make some hot chocolate. Just act normal," she said. "They'll soon lose interest. Absolutely *no one* can hear what I'm about to tell you."

Lena went to the stove and found a pan. She measured out some water and began to heat it up, then spooned hot chocolate powder into four mugs and kneeled down. She was right about the other teams and they went back to chatting between them.

"So where is this … valuable item?" I asked.

"It's not that far at all," said Lena. "In fact, we can get the treasure and *still* complete the weekend. I've mapped out the route and I reckon it'll turn out to be a shortcut. We'll probably save at least a couple of hours of walking."

The water began to boil and Lena poured it into the mugs.

"So what?" said Scarlett. "If we quit we can be on that minibus heading home in a few hours! Or tomorrow morning, at least."

Lena shook her head. "We can't quit. Not now we're so close," she muttered.

"Even if we do go, what if we get lost?" I said.

"We won't!" said Lena. "And it'll be worth it. I promise you."

Josh, who had been silent for a while, sat forward.

"What kind of treasure are we talking about?" he said. "Like gold and stuff?"

Lena grinned. Josh clearly hadn't completely dismissed the idea like Scarlett. Lena stirred the hot chocolates, then handed them to us.

"I can tell you all about it, if you'd like? It's a fascinating story," she said. The mug felt comforting and warm between my palms. I blew on to the hot drink and waited as Lena settled down in front of us.

And then she told us her plan.

"Fortune Mountain has had that name since the seventeenth century. Back then the waters around some parts of the world were extremely dangerous due to the amount of pirates patrolling them. One pirate grew up on the coast just five miles from here."

She paused to take a sip of her drink. I looked at Josh and Scarlett; they were watching Lena, waiting for her to continue. She had us interested, that was for sure.

"This pirate had a fascinating life," continued Lena. "He started out as a sailor who worked on various ships from a young age and travelled all over the world. But when he was around twenty he turned to piracy and became one of the most notorious villains of the time. He looted thousands of pounds' worth of cargo on his ship *The Phantom*."

"What kind of cargo?" said Josh.

"Anything of value. Food, spices, weapons," she said.

"Oh, that's so *boring*," said Josh, sniffing. "I thought you were going to say gold or something."

"Hang on, Josh," said Lena. "I haven't finished yet. This pirate captured a ship in the Red Sea and the cargo was his greatest booty and the best that the crew had ever seen."

"*Now* we're talking," said Josh, his teeth flashing white in the fading light.

"He and his crew escaped back to England. But

183

after that the records become patchy. *The Phantom* apparently sank two years later off the coast of Ireland. There were rumours that one of the crew murdered the captain in his sleep and another rumour said that he escaped capture and lived out his days on an island in the Pacific Ocean. However, one thing that is consistent in all the stories is that he managed to hide his greatest find inside a mountain."

"Fortune Mountain!" said Josh, really getting into it. "The clue is in the name, eh?"

Lena grinned. "Exactly," she said. "No one knows exactly what the item is. Only that it is very valuable indeed."

"What was the pirate's name?" I asked. I blew on my hot chocolate again, then looked over at Lena, whose eyes were twinkling.

"His name was Walter Morgan," she said.

That name was in the title of the book I'd seen on the minibus: *The Life and Escapades of Walter Morgan*.

"I've been doing weeks of research and everything points to the mountain. And I know where to look."

We all sat there for a while, taking in what she'd just told us.

"So, what do you think?" said Lena. "Are you in? Vincent?"

I scratched at the side of my head. "I don't know, Lena," I said. "It all sounds a bit … far-fetched?"

"But it's true!" shouted Lena. She realized she'd raised her voice too much and went back to whispers. "My grandpa had been researching the story about Walter Morgan's hidden treasure for the last twenty years. And just before he died he told me he'd worked out where the entrance to the tunnel is. On the right-hand side of the mountain there is an overhanging rock that looks like a hooked nose."

I twisted round to see if I could spot it but the mountain was in darkness.

"Grandpa studied aerial photography of the area and close to that overhanging rock he spotted some boulders on the ground that appeared to be in the shape of a letter. The letter P. Grandpa thought that the letter P related to Walter's ship, *The Phantom*. He told me he believed that the tail of the P pointed to an entrance into the mountain which leads to a chamber where the treasure is hidden."

We were quiet for a few seconds and then Scarlett began to laugh.

"That is the most ridiculous thing that I have ever heard," said Scarlett. "I'm sorry, Lena. I know you were a big fan of this grandpa of yours, but really? Pirate treasure?"

"It's true!" said Lena.

Josh scrunched up his nose. "Yeah, right," he said. "And this Walter bloke had a wooden leg and a parrot on his shoulder, am I right?"

Lena's face reddened. She looked desperate. "My grandpa knew where to look, but he never got the chance. He has given me the coordinates and it's not far. Vincent? You believe it, don't you?"

I felt sorry for Lena, but I agreed with Josh and Scarlett. It all sounded like the wild imaginings of an old man with too much time on his hands.

"I'm not being rude, but you told us that this grandpa believed in vampires, didn't you?" I said. "Maybe your grandpa was a bit … confused?"

Josh snorted. "Oh, yeah! I remember about the vampires now!" he said. "That was *well* funny."

"Fine," said Lena. "I can see that none of you know the meaning of the word 'team'. I'm going to bed. Goodnight!"

And with that she dropped her mug on to the grass, unzipped her tent and climbed in.

Scarlett and Josh rolled their eyes.

"Well, *that* was interesting," said Scarlett.

"I can't believe she thinks that hidden treasure actually exists. It's like a fairy tale or something!" I said. But I said it quietly in case Lena could hear.

Josh sniffed and cleared his throat. "Maybe it's worth a look, though."

"What?" said Scarlett. "You'd actually wander into a creepy old mountain just because of some bizarre story that is most definitely not true?"

Josh took a long breath, appearing to be thinking about it. "Why not?" he said. "It doesn't look that far away. *And* if we do find anything, it'll be good to see the faces of this lot when we come back with piles of cash!" He nodded his head towards the other teams.

"You're just as deluded as she is!" said Scarlett. "I say let's quit in the morning and go home. I'm off to bed."

She got up and went into the girls' tent. I couldn't imagine they'd be having much of a chat before going to sleep.

"What do you think, Vincent?" said Josh, wiggling his eyebrows. "Fancy a treasure hunt?"

I thought then about how I'd already been treasure hunting with Fabian. I loved looking for clues and solving puzzles that might lead me to finding the gems of the Scorpion Sword. But this was real life, not on a computer screen. And the world worked differently out here. Especially for me.

"No. I don't think so," I said.

Josh shrugged, slurped the last of his drink and then got up.

"Fair enough," he said. "Home it is, then. Night."

"Night."

Josh crawled into our tent and I heard him rustling around as he got into his sleeping bag.

I sat there for a moment and looked up at the black night sky. There was a myriad of stars, twinkling down at me, and the more I looked, the more stars I saw. I suddenly felt very, very small, sitting there beside our tent. I was just a tiny speck in a great, vast universe. Tiny specks didn't do exciting things like go on treasure hunts, did they?

I finished the rest of my hot chocolate and went into my tent, hoping I'd get a decent night's sleep and that it wouldn't be long before I was travelling home.

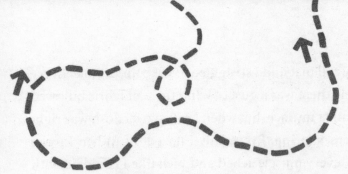

Chapter Twenty-One

Team "Stranded"

I never knew that sleeping out in the wilderness would be so noisy. I was used to the sounds of a town outside my double-glazed bedroom window. I'd maybe hear a few cars driving past and the occasional bark of a dog in the distance. But the countryside had its own orchestra of sounds. I recognized the hooting of an owl, but when I heard a strange noise that sounded like a wild animal being strangled, I prodded Josh awake to see if he'd heard it as well. He mumbled that it was a fox, before disappearing deep inside his sleeping bag. The ground was really hard underneath my roll mat and I struggled to get comfortable. Every time there was a gust of wind the tent fabric billowed against my face, but when I rolled over, Josh was right there, snoring. Eventually I dozed off. When I woke up, every muscle ached and I felt like I could do with another ten hours' sleep. Josh still had his eyes shut and his mouth wide open, so I quietly eased myself out of my sleeping bag and unzipped the tent. The camp was deserted. All the other teams must have packed up and left already. Lena was up and dressed, with her back to me. She hadn't heard I was there and I watched her as she lifted her rucksack on to her shoulders. What was she doing?

"Where are you going, Lena?" I said. She jumped and spun round. The map was dangling around her neck in the plastic wallet.

"I'm going to do what I came for," she said, holding her head high. "Hunt for treasure."

Lena's tent unzipped and Scarlett's head appeared through the flaps.

"Urgh. I thought it was just a bad dream. But I'm still here," she said. She clocked that Lena looked suspiciously like she was about to leave. "What's going on?"

Panic was beginning to rise in my chest. Lena

couldn't go to the mountain on her own, and she couldn't leave us alone either. What was she thinking?

"Lena is heading to the mountain on her own!" I said. "She wants to go and find the treasure."

Scarlett frowned. "So what?" she said. "We were going to quit anyway. She can do what she wants." She stretched her arms and crawled out of the tent. "We'll just tell Dale and Carmen that we're done. No problem."

"Dale and Carmen left when you lot were still sleeping," said Lena bluntly. "Carmen had to get to the first checkpoint to set up. I told them to log our start time in thirty minutes. We haven't got a chance of winning so they didn't seem worried if it wasn't exactly accurate."

She looked at us both, hesitating for a moment, before sticking her thumbs into her rucksack straps and walking off.

"Wait!" I said, stumbling after her in bare feet. "You can't leave us!"

"Let her go," Scarlett called after me. "We'll just use the emergency phone. She won't get far!"

Lena kept walking. "Not if you don't have it any more!" she yelled behind her. "I took it yesterday, remember?"

I trod on a sharp stone and stopped. She hadn't given the phone back to me!

"Quick, Scarlett. We've got to stop her!" I went back to my tent and fumbled trying to get my boots on. The faster I tried, the more complicated it seemed to be.

Lena turned around one last time and hollered: "Just stay there, OK? I won't be long and I'll come back for you!" And she disappeared behind some trees.

Just then the zip of our tent opened. "What's going on?" called Josh. His jet-black hair was sticking up all over the place and he rubbed at his face.

"Everyone has left. Lena has gone off to look for the treasure and taken the emergency phone. We're stranded," I said. I could feel my heart fluttering wildly. "We need to follow her!"

Josh yawned.

"Chill, Vincent," he said. "We know where she's heading. The overhanging rock that looks like a nose, remember?"

"I can't believe she's done this!" said Scarlett. "Come on. If we catch her up, we can get the phone and we won't have to go anywhere near that silly mountain."

*

If we thought putting a tent up was hard, taking it down and making it fit inside a small canvas bag was even harder. Especially when you were in a rush. And the longer it took us, the more agitated Scarlett became.

"You're not folding it tightly enough!" she yelled at me and Josh as we made our third attempt to get ours to fit. "Squeeze it!"

Eventually, we were packed ready to go, even if some of the tents were spilling out of the bags. We walked in the direction that Lena had headed. Fortune Mountain still looked menacing, even in daylight. It seemed to fill the sky completely and I stretched my neck backwards to take it all in. On the side of the mountain was a scorched black tree that must have been struck by lightning. I spotted a large bird with a huge wingspan circling above us. I had the feeling it was watching us, waiting for us to make a mistake before it could strike.

"Is that a vulture?" I asked Josh.

"No," said Josh. "You don't get vultures in this country. That's a buzzard. It's probably looking for its breakfast."

As we walked, I stared up at the bird, watching it gliding on the breeze. It was like it was following us.

"Don't worry. They don't eat humans, you know," said Josh. "We're much too big."

I quickly stopped tracking the bird. "I wasn't worried," I said.

"Yeah, of course you weren't."

It should have been easy to get to where we needed to. It was just a straight line after all, but the pathway soon disappeared and we found ourselves in thick undergrowth and spiky ferns. Josh picked up a stick and walked ahead, slashing it from left to right. When we eventually reached a clearing, Scarlett sank to the floor. "This is so pointless!" she said.

Josh looked just as fed up. "We might have been the worst team here but we *did* have an excellent map reader."

"True," I said. "And she planned to take us on a detour *and* back on the route. I reckon she could have done it too."

"For sure," said Josh. "If I'd woken earlier I would have gone with her to find the treasure."

We were all silent as we contemplated what on earth to do next. Scarlett pulled a twig out of her hair.

"I wish she was here, actually," she mumbled.

We all jumped as a bush beside us began to shake and I waited for a wild animal to burst out.

"It looks like you're in luck," said a voice.

"Lena!" I said. I noticed Scarlett was grinning, but then her face dropped to a scowl.

"How dare you leave us?" said Scarlett. "We could have died!"

"I told you I'd come back for you," said Lena.

"But you took the emergency phone!" I said. "We were stranded."

Lena bit on her lip. "I didn't, actually. I put it back in your rucksack when you were asleep. I wouldn't have taken it, just in case you needed it."

"Didn't you check your bag, Vincent?" said Scarlett. I shrugged. I'd just assumed Lena had been telling the truth. "Right. Get the phone out right now," she said.

I began to take my rucksack off but Lena held up her hand.

"Hang on a minute," said Lena. "Please don't do this. This is the one and only chance that I'll ever have of proving that my grandpa wasn't the fool that everyone believed he was."

"Yes," I said. "We know!"

"Do you, though?" she snapped. "Have you ever wanted to really do something? Been within touching distance of it, only for everyone else to say no?"

I shrugged. "I know how it feels *not* to be able to do something, if that's what you mean," I said. "I've had years of practice."

Lena's face lit up a little. "In that case, wouldn't finding the treasure be something you could do to prove that you *are* capable and that you *can* do things?"

I thought about it for a moment.

"According to *my* brother, *your* brother is brilliant at everything. Is that right?" Lena said.

"I guess," I said. I knew where she was going with this and I wasn't too happy about it.

"Wouldn't it feel great to go home and say to everyone – look what I've found! It would be you who had achieved something amazing. Not Ewan!"

It did sound kind of tempting.

"And you, Scarlett. Don't you want to prove to those other teams that we are capable and we can do something beyond their wildest dreams?" I waited for Scarlett to object, but she didn't.

"It would be good to see their faces if we cross the finish line with a pot of gold or something, I guess. *If* that even exists, of course."

Lena's face broke into a smile.

"Does that mean you're coming?" she said.

Scarlett shrugged. "I'm not doing it for *you*," she snapped. "I'm doing it to get back at *them*. And, if this is a shorter route like you said, it'll get this whole thing over quicker, won't it?"

"We're going treasure hunting!" said Lena, getting to her feet and doing a little jump of excitement. She looked at me. "Isn't that right, Vincent?"

I took a deep breath.

"Come on, Vincent," said Lena. "Let's prove we can do this, shall we?"

I exhaled and groaned a little. "I guess I don't have much choice, do I?" I said. "All right. I'm in."

"Yay!" said Lena. She ran over and patted me on my back.

"You won't regret this. I promise!" she said.

"Hang on a minute," said Josh. "What about me?"

We all looked at him.

"Well?" said Scarlett. "Are you coming or what?"

Josh rubbed his chin as if he was thinking about it, and then he grinned. "Absolutely!"

Chapter Twenty-Two

Thunder on Fortune Mountain

Lena led us through the dense undergrowth on to a woodland path. She seemed confident about which way to go, and I was grateful to have her with us again. The canopies of the trees above us were so thick that not much light was penetrating through. It was cold as well, and the ground was damp and springy underfoot. Josh began to whistle a tune. He was quite good at it, but Scarlett told him to shut up and he went quiet. Suddenly, there was a cracking noise like a large stick had been snapped not far behind us. We all stopped and turned around.

"What was that?" I said. "It sounded like someone stepping on a branch."

We stood, motionless, and listened.

"Hello?" called Lena. "Is someone there?"

A leaf leisurely fluttered down from a tree, and a bush seemed to tremble slightly as if something had jumped into it.

"It was probably just a rabbit or something," said Josh.

"Yeah. Come on," said Scarlett. She carried on walking as we followed.

After about forty minutes we came out of the woodland and the path went left or right. Lena stopped and we grouped together. I looked up at the mountain. It didn't appear to be any closer than when we'd left the camp, but maybe it was my imagination.

Lena studied the map and checked her compass. "We'll head that way, towards the mountain." She pointed to the left. "We'll get the treasure, then go north and rejoin this path a few miles up. Then we can carry on to the third checkpoint."

"The third?" I said. "But what about the first and the second? Won't everyone be worrying if we don't turn up for those?"

Lena chewed on her lip for a moment. "It'll be fine. They will just think we got a bit lost. We'll get there *eventually*."

"Sounds good to me," said Josh, turning left.

We walked beside the tall trees of the woodland that we'd just walked through, and my heart leaped when there was a sudden rapid tapping sound.

"What was that?" I said.

"Relax. It's only a woodpecker," said Josh. "It's drumming on a tree trying to find bugs."

The drumming noise was then followed by a weird chattering sound which echoed around the dark wood.

"Just a woodpecker?!" I said, my blood turning cold. "Someone is laughing at us!"

"That's the woodpecker too!" said Josh. "Although I guess it *could* be a dead pirate following us, worried we are going to steal his treasure. Arrr, me hearties!" He was smirking.

"It's not funny, Josh," I said.

"Yes. Don't be so childish," said Scarlett. She looked a bit freaked too.

"Actually, there *is* a ghost story connected to this area," said Lena. "The legend goes that on certain nights of the year, Walter Morgan can be seen wandering around the mountain, groaning and moaning as he protects his hidden treasure from being found."

Scarlett stopped abruptly.

"And you decide to tell us this, NOW?" she said. "Right. I vote we turn back. I don't want to bump into any ghost pirate."

"It's just a story, Scarlett," said Lena.

"Well, what times of the year is he seen here? Is it this time of the year?"

"I don't know," said Lena. "Maybe?"

"Chill!" said Josh. "The noise in the wood was just a rabbit or a squirrel and that laughing was a yaffle."

"A yaffle?" I said. "Is it some kind of animal?"

Josh found that hilarious. "No. A yaffle is a woodpecker's call."

"I don't know what I'm more surprised about. The fact that there might be a pirate ghost wandering around, or the fact Josh Park is an expert on nature. Where did you learn this stuff?" said Scarlett.

Josh shrugged.

"Is it your hobby?" said Lena. "Do you go bird watching?"

Josh screwed up his nose. "Nah," he said. "I can't be bothered."

I remembered what he'd told me about his dad selling his binoculars. Maybe what had happened had put him off going out and seeing nature rather than just reading about it in a book.

"Maybe you could volunteer or something?" said Lena. "There must be loads of wildlife charities around."

Josh shrugged again, but he didn't say no.

We carried on walking for another hour or so and we fell into a comfortable rhythm. I thought it felt a bit like we were becoming a team at last, heading for a secret mission. I didn't say anything to the others, though, in case they laughed at me. We went through another dark canopy of trees and emerged on to some open scrubland. There were large boulders all around us with the pathway leading between them. We turned left around one of the boulders, and then Lena stopped and tilted her head upwards. We stood beside her.

"Here we are," said Lena, slightly breathless. "Fortune Mountain."

In front of us was the steep rockface of the almighty mountain. Now we were closer I could see even more colours amongst the shades of green and brown, and a steep pathway snaked its way up the side, disappearing behind some trees.

"Is it me or is it like … it's alive?" said Josh. He immediately flushed, probably thinking it sounded odd, but I knew exactly what he meant.

"It's like a giant," I said.

"Silently watching and waiting for something to happen," whispered Scarlett. I shivered.

The wind began to pick up, and behind us the clouds were a dark, purply grey. There was a low rumble of thunder. The kind that made your ribs feel like they were vibrating in your chest.

"It sounds like Walter Morgan is angry that we are getting closer," said Josh quietly.

"Let's get moving," said Lena. We followed her as she made her way between the boulders, stopping every so often to check the route. The wind was getting much stronger now and she struggled to read the map as it flapped around in front of her face. It began to spit with rain and I pulled my hood up. A flash of lightning lit up the ground around us, followed by a huge crack of thunder that made us all jump.

"Shouldn't we take shelter?" I said. But Lena carried on walking. The rain began to fall heavily and it wasn't long before we were walking in a deluge.

It poured off my hood and in front of my face like a waterfall.

Josh was beside me. "I really don't think we should be walking in this, do you?" I yelled at him. It was hard to be heard above the wind, rain and rumbles of thunder.

He nodded and pointed to some boulders which leaned against each other and had a narrow groove in between them. We could hide in the gap to shelter. Scarlett followed me and Josh ran up to Lena to tell her to turn back and join us. Inside the crevice it was cold and dark but at least it was dry. I took my hood down.

Josh dived in beside us but Lena hovered by the entrance.

"We need to keep going!" she said.

"Let's just wait here until the worst of it passes," I said.

Lena hesitated for a moment, and then there was another big crackle of lightning and a rumble of thunder and she hurried into the gap.

"We can't wait too long or we'll be behind schedule," she said.

We rummaged in our bags to find something to eat and drink. We were all hungry from missing breakfast. I stared out of the crevice at the rain hitting the ground and sipped on my water. It was so dark it felt like evening rather than late morning. Another great flash of lightning lit up the pathway and, in that brief second, I saw something. There was a figure standing on the other side of the path.

"There's someone out there!" I gasped.

Lena squeezed beside me. "Where?" she said.

I pointed. "There! There was someone standing right there!"

We peered into the gloom and Josh and Scarlett squashed in behind us.

"It's the pirate ghost!" said Scarlett.

Another flash lit the sky and I recoiled. But this time the path was empty. Whatever I'd seen had gone.

"There's no one there," said Lena. "You must have imagined it."

"I didn't!" I said. "There was a man standing right there! Well, I think it was a man. I only saw their back. They were looking towards the mountain."

"It's Walter Morgan, warning us to stay away from his treasure!" said Josh. And then he did a silly, moaning noise.

"Stop it, Josh. I'm being serious," I said. I turned to Lena.

"Does anyone else know about the treasure?" I

asked. "Maybe someone is trying to find it as well?"

She shook her head.

"No. Only me and Grandpa know about the entrance." She peered out and up at the sky.

"The rain is easing off. We need to get moving again," she said.

"But what about the figure I saw? Maybe we should wait for a bit. Just to be certain that they've gone."

"There was no one there, Vincent," said Lena. "Come on. We can't afford to take too long."

Scarlett pushed past me. "Let's just get on with it," she said. "Come on."

We headed out of our shelter and back to the path. I had definitely seen someone. Hadn't I? I checked up ahead and then looked in the direction that we'd just come from. There was no one there. Maybe it had just been a trick of the light?

"Come on, Vincent," called Josh. "Stop worrying!"

I sighed and began to follow them as more thunder rumbled in the distance.

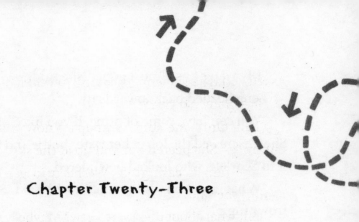

Chapter Twenty-Three

Lena the Map Reader

Lena spent a lot longer looking at the map than she had done yesterday, but after each check she said, "It's this way," with such confidence that I didn't think about it too much.

It was still raining steadily and the blister on my foot was really hurting again. After half an hour of walking, Scarlett stopped. Lena was way up in front and Scarlett yelled out to her.

"Stop, Lena! I need a drink." She shuffled out of her rucksack, got her water bottle and took a long swig. She shook the bottle. It sounded nearly empty.

"My water has almost gone," she said.

Lena headed back towards us.

"You can have some of mine, if you like," she said. She unscrewed the top of her water bottle and handed it to Scarlett, who looked bewildered.

"What are you doing that for?" said Scarlett, frowning.

"What am I doing what for?" said Lena.

Scarlett nodded towards her bottle. "Sharing your water. Have you spat in it or something?"

Scarlett actually thought that Lena would do that to her?

"Erm, no," said Lena. "I've got nearly a full bottle of water so I thought you could have some of mine. That's all. It's called being *nice*."

Scarlett frowned. "Is there dirt in it, then? Or a dead fly?"

Before I thought about what I was doing, I opened my mouth. "Not everyone is horrible like you, you know, Scarlett."

Her head whipped round and she faced me. "What did you say?" She glared at me and I swallowed. I hadn't meant to say it out loud.

"I was just saying that not everyone is horrible. Sometimes people do nice things for no reason."

Scarlett took a deep breath. "Not in my world," she muttered.

I thought about her mum, who seemed to be quite hard on her. And her friends didn't seem to be the nicest either. I thought of my dad and what kind of thing he would say right now. I wasn't sure how to say it like Dad, but I gave it a go.

"I guess if you're surrounded by angry people, like, um, an angry parent or something, then being angry yourself is kind of like your armour. Like a way of protecting yourself," I said.

Scarlett shrugged. "I … I guess. But maybe some people don't really realize they take stuff out on you. Maybe they're *permanently* angry and stressed with work and it's become like a habit or something."

Her cheeks flushed and I wondered if she had meant to blurt all of that out. I thought she might be talking about her mum.

"Well, in that case, I'd say it might be a good idea to tell that person how you feel. Perhaps?"

Scarlett stared at the ground, blinking. I hoped she was thinking over what I'd said. She turned back to Lena.

"I'll just take a little bit, then," she said. She took Lena's bottle and tipped a small amount into her own.

"You can have more than that, if you want," said Lena. "I've got loads."

Scarlett frowned again, but then she tipped more in and handed the bottle back. This was clearly a whole new experience for her.

"Thanks," she muttered.

Josh was sitting down on a rock and I went to sit beside him. I needed to take a look at my foot before we walked any further. I undid the clips on my boots. I could sense that the others were watching me, probably wondering why I didn't have laces like everyone else. I pulled my boot off and carefully peeled my sock down.

"Urgh, that is DISGUSTING," said Josh. The back of my left heel was raw, red flesh – it looked much worse than it had last night. The blister must have burst and the raw skin had been rubbing against my boot. No wonder it was so painful. I felt a bit sick looking at it.

Scarlett stood in front of me with her hand on her hips.

"I can … um … I can help you with that, if you'd like," she said.

"Help me?" I asked.

She looked embarrassed. "Yeah. It needs cleaning.

Otherwise you might get an infection. And I can dress it. Then it won't hurt so much."

I was so stunned I just stared back at her, speechless.

"Unless you *want* to be in pain?" she snapped. She waited for a moment, then went to pick up her rucksack. "Oh, forget it," she said. I edged forward on the rock.

"Yes, please. That would be great! Thanks, Scarlett." I looked sideways at Lena, who raised her eyebrows at me.

Scarlett got her first-aid kit from her bag and kneeled down beside my foot. She didn't seem bothered by the wound at all and she dabbed at it with some antiseptic wipes. It hurt, but it didn't take her long and she covered it with a large plaster.

"How do you know what to do?" said Josh.

Scarlett carried on working on my foot. "I went to Brownies when I was little," she said. "I got my stage five first-aid badge."

I couldn't imagine Scarlett doing anything that involved caring for someone else, but then we were finding out more about each other by the minute. Scarlett secured the plaster with some extra tape to help keep it in place.

"That should feel a bit better," she said as she put

her kit away. I just sat there with my foot dangling in her face. She looked up at me.

"I'm not putting your sock back on for you if that's what you're waiting for," she said, but there was a flicker of a smile on her face.

"Oh, right," I said. "Sure." I rummaged around in my bag and found another clean pair of socks.

Josh climbed up on to the boulder we were sitting on and took a look around.

"It looks a bit rough up ahead," he said. "Is the giant rock nose that way?"

"Yes," said Lena. "We're nearly there."

Once I had my boot back on we set off again. 'A bit rough' was a major understatement. There was no obvious path to follow and we spent the next hour clambering over rocks, wading through long grass, and battling our way through lots of sharp, scratchy bushes. One section was so overgrown it felt like we were swimming through brambles. Scarlett yelped as she got scratched across her cheek.

"We had better be nearly there, Lena!" she yelled. "This is awful!"

I held my arm up to try and shield my face from as much as I could, but I was still getting thorns in my hands and hair.

Lena stopped walking and stared at the map again and held her compass out. From where we were standing the pathway went left or right.

"Which way, then?" said Josh. This time Lena seemed a bit more hesitant to make a decision. She turned right and looked down the path, then turned left and stared that way.

"Is everything OK?" I asked, slightly worried.

Lena nodded. "Yep," she said. She consulted the map again, then seemed to gain confidence. "It's this way." She marched left.

"Isn't that the way we've just come from?" I asked, worried.

Lena kept on walking. "Grandpa's coordinates are in that direction. I must have missed the overhanging rock. Once we've found that we will see the boulders in the shape of a P, which will point us to the entrance."

I was too tired to argue and I think Scarlett and Josh felt the same, so we just put our heads down and ploughed on.

The rain became heavy again and before long we were walking in another torrential downpour. I checked my watch and my heart sank. We'd been walking for hours and there was still no sign of Lena's mysterious mountain entrance. I had an awful feeling that things were going very, very badly and Lena was just too embarrassed, or too proud, to admit it. She kept walking way out in front of us, but she was starting to slow down. Josh walked beside me and we were both silent – too tired to speak. Scarlett was in front of us and I noticed her stagger slightly.

"Lena?" I called. "I think we need to stop and have a break."

Josh, Scarlett and I went and stood underneath a pine tree to shelter from the rain. Lena was still peering at her map and turning it around in her hands.

"What are you looking for?" yelled Josh.

Lena came over to us, an anguished expression on her face.

"I'm trying to find some landmarks," she said. "We're definitely on the right route, but I can't quite place where the entrance is."

"We've been walking for *hours*," said Scarlett. "Let's just give up."

"No! We just need to find the hooked rock then we'll be fine," Lena said.

"Will we, though?" I said. "Even if we find this entrance, what if we can't get in? It could be blocked or something." I was also quite worried that it would be really dark and scary inside a mountain.

"It'll be fine," said Lena. "Come on."

She folded up her map and began to walk again. Scarlett groaned.

The three of us reluctantly traipsed after Lena. The rain poured, and the path twisted and turned, and we put our heads down and kept walking on and on and on. The only one who didn't seem to be struggling was Josh. He caught up with Lena and said something to her, then she unclipped the tent from her rucksack and gave it to him. He was now carrying both of the tents. I was just grateful he hadn't handed ours back to me.

Eventually, the path we were following came to an abrupt end and we were faced with a giant boulder. Lena stood in front of it, looking upwards.

"Now what do we do?" said Scarlett.

I checked my watch again. It was getting late and daylight was beginning to fade. We were running out of energy and we were all soaked to the skin. Ms Bell, Mr Hearn and the Wilderness Warriors team must be really worried about us by now.

"Lena?" I said. "What do we do? We can't get over that."

She turned and walked back to us.

"I've got something I want to say," she said. She stood in front of us, the rain dripping off the brim of her hat. Her forehead crumpled and my stomach flipped over. This wasn't going to be good.

"Well, go on, then," said Josh. "What is it?"

"I'm really sorry but," she began, "I think we might be lost."

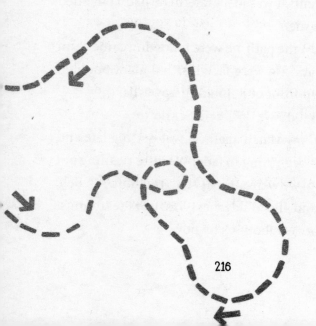

Chapter Twenty-Four

A Night on Our Own

"We are WHAT?" screeched Scarlett, suddenly getting her energy back. "What do you mean we are LOST?"

Just then there was another low rumble of thunder. It sounded like something deep inside the great mountain was grumbling.

"Where's the tunnel, Lena?" yelled Josh. "You *promised* that this would be a shortcut!"

"I know. And I'm sorry," said Lena, close to tears. She held the map up. "It's here somewhere, I just know it. But I ... I can't find it."

I noticed then that she was using the yellow map she'd bought in the motorway services and not the one the school had given us.

"What about the other map?" I said, feeling desperate. "Is that more useful?"

Lena shook her head. "No. That one doesn't cover this area at all."

"Well, in that case, we need to use the emergency phone," I said. I put my rucksack down and fiddled with the fastenings.

"No!" shouted Lena. "We can't do that! We are so close!"

"Lena, we're *lost*," said Scarlett. "There's another storm coming, we are running out of water and I for one don't want to spend a night out here on our own. That mountain is giving me the creeps."

I knew what she meant. I could feel the mountain there, observing our every move. I plunged my hand into my bag and felt the plastic wallet deep at the bottom. I took it out.

"*Please* don't use the phone, Vincent," said Lena. "Let's set up camp here and if we can't find the tunnel entrance in the morning, *then* we call."

"Sleep out here on our own?" said Scarlett. "No way! Make the call, Vincent."

I held the seal, ready to break it, when Lena grabbed my arm.

"Hang on!" she said, her eyes wide. "If you break that seal then this whole thing is over, remember?"

"So what?" said Scarlett. "It's all been a waste of time anyway. Just open it."

I couldn't grip the seal tightly enough to break it and when I tried again, Lena cried out.

"NO! STOP!"

She looked desperate.

"Just stop for a second and think about it, please, Vincent?"

I waited. Lena took a deep breath.

"If you make a call then we have all failed. And isn't that what everyone expects us to do? All those other teams at the camp last night were laughing at us. You all saw it! If we make that call, then they'll think it's funny that we've lived up to what they were calling us – Team Useless?"

Josh sniffed. "They were pretty rude about my trainers," he said. He turned to me. "And they laughed at you too, Vincent. I'm sure they would just love to know we got lost."

"But everyone will be worrying about us," I said.

Scarlett huffed. "I seriously doubt that," she

muttered. I wasn't sure if she was referring to the teachers or her family.

Lena turned to Scarlett.

"So you agree with me?" she said. "We should camp here tonight?"

Scarlett shrugged. "Oh, I don't know. Yes?" she said. "I don't want everyone thinking we're losers."

Lena smiled and turned to Josh. "And you don't want to be known as Team Useless any more, do you, Josh?"

Josh paused. "Nope. One night won't hurt, I guess."

The three of them looked at me. After all, I was the one still holding the phone. It was my decision what we did next.

"Vincent?" said Lena.

I thought how everyone would be anxious about what had happened to us, but then I also knew how humiliating it would be to make that call and have to get picked up. And not only that, we'd probably be in a load of trouble for going off-route as well. I looked around to make sure we weren't being watched. I didn't see anyone.

"How close do you think we are to the treasure?" I said. "*If* it actually exists in the first place."

Lena fumbled with the map and stood beside me.

"The entrance is in this area here," she said, circling her finger around a small section of the map. "And I am pretty certain that we are right in the centre of that."

It did look like we were close.

"So why haven't we found it?" I said.

"I don't know. I've been using Grandpa's coordinates but it's been no use. I think we'll have to look for a rock in the shape of a P. *Then* we'll see exactly where the entrance is."

I sighed.

"OK," I said. "But I'm not happy about it."

Lena gasped. "That's brilliant, Vincent!" she said. "Thank you. You won't regret it, I promise."

I felt like I already was.

"So, now what do we do?" said Scarlett. "Get a hotel room, have a nice hot shower and a big roast dinner?"

My stomach rumbled at the thought of food. I was absolutely starving again.

"Let's set up camp and get something cooking. We'll all feel better once we've eaten. Then tomorrow we can get up early, find the entrance, get the treasure and be back on track before the other teams have even set off."

Lena made it sound quite straightforward and I felt myself relax ever so slightly. Although I wasn't sure how we were going to cook anything with the rain coming down.

Lena led us to a clearing not far from the base of the mountain, and we managed to put the tents up in record time. Lena lit the camp stove, and Josh tipped some sachets of flavoured rice into a pan. I felt cold now that we were sitting down and I started to shiver.

"We should change into dry clothes," said Scarlett. "We don't want to get pneumonia or something."

She dived into her tent and Josh went into ours to change while Lena stirred the rice. When it was my turn I put a few extra layers on. The rain had stopped and I sat at the front of our tent and wrapped my arms around my knees. It was dusk and I spotted some shapes flitting around just above our heads.

"There's something out there!" I said.

"It's just bats," said Josh. "They won't bother us. They're just feeding on the bugs. They're doing us a favour really. Less chance of us getting bitten."

I watched the bats scooting and flapping around us, ducking this way and that and somehow avoiding crashing into anything, or each other.

"Right. Who's ready to eat?" said Lena. Josh handed out the plates and Lena came over with the pan and dropped a dollop of rice on to each one. It steamed in front of my face and smelled wonderful.

"It's a shame we can't light a fire," said Lena. "But any wood we find now will be utterly soaked."

I blew on a forkful of rice and began to eat. It tasted fantastic. Dad was right. Food cooked outside did taste extra special.

Scarlett looked up at the side of the mountain.

"What I don't understand is, if there *is* some treasure, why didn't Walter come back for it?" she said. "Or one of his crew. Someone must have known where he'd hidden it."

Lena shook her head. "Not necessarily. He wouldn't have trusted anyone. These were pirates, remember? They didn't have any real loyalty to one another. And pirates would do anything to avoid getting captured because they knew that if they did, well, let's just say it was very unpleasant."

I didn't really want to know what was unpleasant about being a captured pirate, but apparently Josh did.

"Go on, then," he said. "What happened if they got caught?"

Lena scraped the rice around her plate, then put her fork down.

"Back in the seventeenth century there used to be some gallows at the edge of the River Thames in London where they would hang convicted pirates. They would leave the corpse dangling for everyone to see until three tides had past. Sometimes they even coated the corpse in tar to preserve it for as long as possible, and they'd display it in an iron gibbet or cage."

"Urgh," said Scarlett. "And anybody could just walk past and see it there?"

"Yep," said Lena. "They thought it would put anyone else off becoming a pirate."

"That's disgusting," said Scarlett.

"It'd put me off, for sure," said Josh, finishing his rice and putting his plate on the ground.

I felt my stomach knot.

"Can we change the subject, please?" I said.

"I agree," said Scarlett. "What else shall we talk about?"

We were all quiet for a moment and then Josh cleared his throat.

"So, why are you lot here, then?" he said.

"What do you mean?" said Lena. "We're here

because the school asked us, aren't we?"

"Well, yeah. But the teachers picked us for a reason, didn't they? I mean, I know that I'm here because everyone thinks I'm a pain in the butt. But what made the school choose the rest of you?"

"You're not a pain in the butt, Josh," I said.

Scarlett laughed. "Yes, he is! He's always messing around. Why *do* you mess around so much?"

Josh raised his eyebrows. "I dunno," he said. "People like people who are funny, don't they? I guess that's why. I'm only trying to have a laugh."

I hadn't thought about it like that. Was Josh just trying to be … entertaining? Didn't he realize the pranks he pulled weren't that amusing?

"I think you are more funny when you're just being yourself," I said.

Josh screwed his nose up. "You what?" he said.

"Yeah, Vincent's right," said Scarlett. "You need to stop all that silly stuff. You are *way* nicer to be around when you're not being an idiot."

Josh laughed. "Er, thanks? I think." He shook his head, a bit bewildered, and then he turned to Lena. "So, what about you, Lena? Why are you here?"

I assumed it was because she was picked on at school. Although how she *and* Scarlett wound up on the same team was a bit of a puzzle. Maybe the school thought that forcing them to spend time together would sort things out? Or maybe the school didn't even realize.

"I asked to come," said Lena. "When I heard where the walk was I had to be here so I could get the chance to investigate Walter Morgan's lost treasure for Grandpa."

"And the school just said you could?" I asked.

"Kind of," said Lena. "When I heard who else was coming I said that maybe it would be good for me to … face up to those who seem to want to bring me down all the time. They fell for that one. They thought I was being brave and stuff."

Her eyes darted over to Scarlett. I wondered if Scarlett was going to say something, but she suddenly seemed very interested in folding the top of her socks over.

No one said anything for a bit and then Josh spoke again.

"And what about you, Scarlett? Why did the school make you come on this trip?"

Scarlett frowned. "I'm not sure," she said, still fiddling with her sock.

"You must have some idea," said Josh.

Scarlett looked really uncomfortable and, although she probably deserved it, I didn't like seeing her look like that.

"Maybe it was a chance to see that sometimes it's easier to be nice than it is to be horrible," said Lena. A day ago Scarlett would have exploded at her, but instead she seemed to be thinking about it.

"Maybe," she said. She took a long breath. "Anyway. You're next, Vincent. Why are you here?"

All three of them waited to see what I was going to say.

"Well," I began, "I guess you've noticed that I'm kind of quiet at school."

Scarlett nodded. "You're practically invisible, Vincent!"

I smiled when she said it this time. Things were changing between the four of us and I knew she didn't mean it rudely.

"I think the teachers thought it would be a good way for me to make friends. I don't have any, you see. Not really."

Josh snorted. "Sorry you got lumbered with us, mate," he said.

"So why don't you have any friends?" said Scarlett. "Do you have a body odour problem or something? I can't say I've noticed it. Yet."

I felt my throat clench a little. I didn't want to mention how I felt incredibly small and insignificant sometimes. Or that I'd spent the last thirteen years living in my brother's shadow. After all, it wasn't his fault he was brilliant at everything.

"I like to keep my head down, I suppose," I said. "I ... I don't feel confident about myself a lot of the time."

"Because of that dyspraxia thing you've got?" asked Scarlett.

"Partly, I guess. But there are other reasons. I'm shy too and it's just easier being on my own."

I glanced at Lena, who was looking at me with concern on her face.

"Anyway, let's talk about something else, shall we?" I said. "What do you think—"

I stopped.

There was the sound of some pebbles scattering down the side of the mountain. It was like someone was walking there and had disturbed them.

"What was that?" said Scarlett. We all stood up.

"I told you someone was following us!" I said.

"It's Walter, I tell you," said Josh, actually sounding scared this time. "We're done for!"

Seeing Josh frightened made me feel even worse. I

had visions of a decaying pirate, staggering out from behind the boulder, running towards us with his cutlass held aloft.

Scarlett had got her torch out and she waved it in the direction of the noise.

"Hello!" called Scarlett. "Who's there? We aren't scared, you know!"

The torchlight was quite weak, but there was a flash of two red eyes and Scarlett yelped.

"It's him! It's the pirate!" she squealed.

We were all paralysed for what felt like ages but must have only been a few seconds. Josh took Scarlett's torch and pointed it towards where the eyes had been, and he breathed a huge sigh of relief.

"It's just a deer!" he said. "A little muntjac. Look!"

The deer was about the size of a very large dog and had reddish-brown fur. Its black nose twitched as it tried to smell us, and its eyes looked red in the torchlight. It didn't seem bothered by us at all and, after a moment, carried on its way.

"I think we'd better try to get some sleep," said Lena. "We have an early start tomorrow."

Scarlett yawned and we all agreed. We got ready for bed and crawled into our sleeping bags, exhausted from the day.

As I lay there and listened to the sounds of the night and Josh snoring, I tried to stop myself from imagining a pirate ghost prowling around outside. Maybe Walter was angry with us for getting so close to his treasure? I'd seen something similar in *Battle Doom* when Fabian had disturbed a knight's tomb in a cathedral on his quest to find the ruby stone. The knight had appeared from behind a giant pillar. His wispy ghostly body and his angry sunken eyes had haunted my nightmares for days. It was scary enough confronting a ghost in a computer game. I really didn't fancy meeting one in real life.

I shut my eyes tightly and waited for sleep to come.

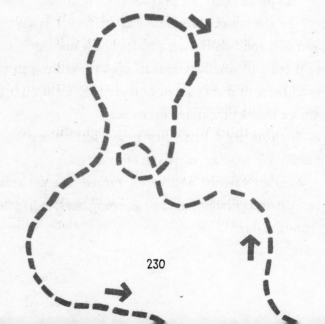

Chapter Twenty-Five

R.I.C.E.

I woke in the very early hours to the distant *thud, thud, thud* of a helicopter's blades. My stomach knotted. Were they searching for us? I felt terrible knowing how everyone would be worrying. It really was a ridiculous decision to stay here overnight. Josh unzipped his sleeping bag.

"Do you think we're doing the right thing, Josh?" I asked.

Josh looked serious for a change.

"We've come this far. We might as well take a look, and if there's nothing, then we make a call? I'm going for a wee." He fumbled out of his sleeping bag and made his way to the tent entrance, accidentally treading on me in the process.

I got dressed and took the emergency mobile out of my rucksack. Maybe I should just call and tell them that we were all OK, then hang up again? That might give us time to get into the mountain so that Lena could look for her treasure before they traced us. I decided to think about it and stuffed the phone into my jacket pocket before going outside. The morning was chilly but at least it was dry. I looked up at Fortune Mountain. The sunlight was reflecting off some of the rocks, making them glint, and I could see that the dark buzzard was back circling overhead.

Lena and Scarlett were already up, and there was a saucepan of porridge bubbling away on the camping stove. I packed my things and went over.

"Morning," I said.

"Morning," said Lena. She looked nervous but excited. I guessed this was a big day for her – the day she'd hopefully prove that her grandpa had been right all along.

We quickly ate our porridge, and as we packed up there was the sound of another helicopter circling not far away. We froze and looked at each other.

"Let's hurry up," said Lena. Josh and I took our tent down and I helped Josh to roll it up as tightly as we could. He then managed to squeeze it into the little bag. We were getting quicker each time.

We loaded ourselves up and set off. My shoulders ached and my foot was hurting again. The plaster must have slipped when I put my boot on and I could feel it clumped under my heel. But there was no time to redress it now.

Lena said we should walk to the left and after ten minutes, Josh suddenly stopped, pointed to the mountain and bellowed, "Hooked nose ahoy!"

Lena squealed with delight and Scarlett clapped her hands together. Up on the mountainside was a large overhanging rock that did indeed look like a nose. It even had two dark hollows like nostrils.

"Brilliant!" said Lena. "Now, are the boulders in a P-shape?" She climbed up on to a large rock and looked around.

"We can walk across these," she said. "It's easier to see their shapes from up here." She began to explore around her.

Josh and Scarlett followed Lena, easily clambering up, but I found it more difficult. I wasn't good with balance as it was, and having a heavy rucksack on my back made it ten times worse. I was scrambling my feet to find a footing when a hand appeared beside my face.

"Here. Hold on to me and it'll be much easier," said Josh.

I grabbed his hand and he helped me up.

"Thanks," I said.

Under foot the rock surface was very uneven and I had to go slowly and steadily. There were boulders all around us and a pathway seemed to meander between them like a maze, but we had to stay up where we were if we had any chance of spotting the tunnel entrance. There weren't any grouped together like a P that I could see. Lena stepped across the boulders and we followed her.

"If it's an entrance to a tunnel then it's probably going to be even closer to the base of the mountain, isn't it?" I said.

"Yes," said Lena. "Let's get a bit nearer."

We carried on but I was finding it quite treacherous work and even Scarlett slipped, banging her knee. I could tell that she was in a lot of pain, but she didn't make much of it and insisted that we carry on. I was slower than everyone else, but they patiently waited for me to catch up and after about fifteen minutes of clambering and climbing we were right by the foot of the mountain, close enough to almost reach out a hand and touch it. I looked up at the steep side and felt incredibly small in comparison. Lena took a few steps to the right and she gasped.

"There! I see them!" she called. She twisted round to us. "Those rocks are in a P-shape and I can see a dark entrance beyond it! We found it!" But as she turned back she seemed to lose her balance. She put her arms out to steady herself but it was no good. She let out a squeal as she toppled over the side of the boulder.

"LENA!" called Scarlett, hurrying to where she'd fallen and jumping down off the side.

Josh followed and I hurried behind them. I dropped down too and tumbled to the ground. Lena was holding her right forearm with her left hand. Her wrist looked red and swollen. All of the blood seemed to have drained from her face, and she was clearly in a lot of pain.

"It's just a sprain. I'm sure of it," said Lena. Her face didn't look so convinced, though.

Scarlett was already rummaging in her rucksack and she pulled out her first-aid kit, just like she had when she'd seen my blister. But Lena's injury looked far worse.

"OK," said Scarlett. "Vincent, can you help Lena take her jacket off? We need to think R.I.C.E. here."

Josh frowned as he joined us. "I don't think now is the time to start cooking, Scarlett."

I held Lena's jacket as she carefully pulled her arm through, wincing slightly. Scarlett unzipped her first-aid kit and took out a small blue-and-white pouch.

"R.I.C.E. is an acronym. The letters stand for the things you should do with an injury like this. The R is for rest. So try not to move your arm from now on, Lena. OK?"

Lena nodded. Scarlett seemed to be really comfortable taking charge of the situation. She squeezed the blue-and-white pouch and began to shake it.

"I stands for ice," she said. She placed the pouch on Lena's wrist and Lena put her other hand on top of it. "This is an ice pack so hold it there for a few minutes. It will help with the swelling and the pain."

She went back to her kit and took out a bandage.

"C stands for compression. I'm going to put this bandage around the wrist to stabilize it; it should help with the pain."

Lena nodded.

We watched as Scarlett opened out a triangular-shaped piece of fabric.

"And finally the E stands for elevation," she said. "When we've iced and wrapped it, I'll make you a sling so it's resting high against your shoulder."

I noticed Lena had a bit more colour in her cheeks as she let Scarlett look after her. We were quiet while she worked. She seemed almost like a professional.

"How does that feel?" said Scarlett.

"Better," said Lena. She awkwardly got to her feet. "Let's go."

"What are you talking about?" I said. "You can't carry on now. You need to go to hospital and get your arm X-rayed. We need to phone Mr Hearn and Ms Bell!"

"I'm not giving up now. *Please?*" said Lena. "It won't take long. We can call them when we come out."

I wasn't happy about this at all. If something happened to us inside the mountain we'd never be found. Scarlett finished tying the sling at the back of Lena's neck and Josh picked up Lena's rucksack. I held out her jacket and she put one arm through the sleeve and I put the other over her shoulder.

"So the plan is to go inside the cave, fill our

pockets with as many pieces of eight, or whatever it is, that we can carry and then come straight out. Yes?" said Josh.

"Absolutely," said Lena, now with a smile on her face.

"And then we will phone Ms Bell. Agreed?" I said.

"She said so, didn't she, Vincent?" said Scarlett. "Chill."

Lena smiled at her. "Thank you for coming with me. I really appreciate it," she said. "I can't imagine doing this on my own."

"That's OK," said Scarlett. "We're a team, aren't we?"

"Yeah, Team Useless!" said Josh, rolling his eyes.

"I think we should do away with that nickname now, don't you?" I said. "How about ... The Treasure Hunters?"

Lena grinned.

"I like it," she said. "Come on, then, Treasure Hunters. Let's go!"

The three of us made our way to the tunnel entrance. It reminded me of a stretched, gaping mouth stretched in an agonized scream, and as soon as I'd pictured that I wished I could have erased it from my mind. I was suddenly really scared. I was about to suggest that maybe this wasn't a good idea after all, when something happened that we really didn't see coming; something that shocked all of us to our core. A person stepped out and stood in front of the gaping hole, their muscular arms folded across their chest.

"Dale!" gasped Lena. "W-what are you doing here?"

"I've been following you the whole time," said Dale. His forehead was furrowed, his eyebrows knitted together.

"The *whole* time?" said Scarlett. "Why haven't you stopped us?"

Dale's face relaxed into a smile, but there was something sinister about it. He had a radio clipped to his waistband and Carmen's voice crackled out of the tiny speaker.

"Dale! Dale! Are you there? Have you had any sightings yet? Over." She sounded desperate and worried, and I instantly felt guilty.

Dale looked at the four of us in a slow, controlled manner, unclipped the radio and pressed the talk button on the side.

"Hi, Carmen. No sign of Team Linley at all, I'm afraid. I think we might have to expect the worst.

239

Over," he said. He held the radio in his hand and then he twisted a little dial and it clicked off. What was he *doing*?

"Now," he said, taking a step towards us. "Let's have a little chat, shall we?"

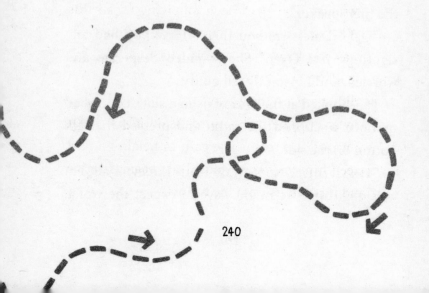

Chapter Twenty-Six

A Light Bulb Moment

"I don't understand," said Lena. "W-what is going on?"

We all looked at each other, baffled. I couldn't think straight. Dale had been following us all this time? Why hadn't he told anyone or stopped us?

"It was you I saw in the storm," I said. "I didn't imagine it!"

He didn't say anything.

"Why are you being all weird?" said Josh. "What do you want?" He seemed to gain in height and I'd never seen him look so serious. Dale began to pace back and forth in front of the tunnel.

"I want you to do a little job for me," he said.

"What kind of job?" said Scarlett.

"Well, your friend Lena Kaminski, here, has been very helpful in a little … mission I've been on for the last year or so. She's helped so much already." He turned to Lena. "Or, should I say, your grandpa has. Which is incredible, really, considering what a pathetic man he was."

"How dare you speak about my grandpa like that!" said Lena. "You never knew him!"

"Not directly, thank goodness," said Dale, inspecting his nails. "But I *do* know he was too weak to be a winner. Dad said he was incapable of understanding how rich he could have been! I mean … what a loser, eh?"

Dale laughed.

"Hang on. I know who you are!" said Lena. "You're Bernie's son!"

Dale didn't react.

"Who on earth is Bernie?" said Scarlett.

I remembered everything Lena had told me on the minibus on the way here.

"Bernie was Lena's grandpa's partner," I said. "They were a team and investigated things together."

242

"Until Grandpa realized that Bernie was only interested in one thing. Money," said Lena. "He wanted to fake things and con people!"

Dale grinned. "What's wrong with that?"

Josh suddenly moved towards Dale and squared up to him. I'd never realized how brave Josh was.

"Whoa, don't try and be a hero now," said Dale, holding up his hands. "You're not exactly the picture of fitness, are you? In fact, I'm quite confident I could take you *all* on."

Josh was tall, but he didn't look muscly like Dale.

"What is *wrong* with you?" shouted Scarlett.

Dale turned his attention to her. "What is *wrong* with me is that I've been stuck in this job for far too long looking after little brats like you, and it wasn't part of my plan!" he said. "Do you have any idea just how *exhausting* it is? Do you think I want to spend my days listening to a bunch of teenagers moaning about walking and carrying a tent and, '*Oh, help me, Dale, I really don't know how to warm up my baked beans.*' Well, I don't. I'm sick of it! And that treasure is my exit plan."

I was beginning to piece everything together.

"So, your dad told you all about Walter Morgan's loot being in Fortune Mountain, then you got a job here so you could try and find it?" I said.

"Bingo," said Dale. "And Lena here blabbed all over the internet that her grandpa had made a big breakthrough on his final mission."

"My blog piece!" said Lena.

"Yes, your blog piece!" mimicked Dale. "Of course, only me and Dad knew that you were talking about Walter's lost treasure. From then on I've kept a very close eye on you."

"Hang on a minute," said Scarlett. "How did you know Lena was going to be here? Isn't it a bit of a coincidence?"

Dale seemed particularly pleased about this next part.

"Remember the school that had dropped out of coming this weekend at the last minute?" he said, grinning. "Their absence conveniently left a space for me to invite *your* school to sign up."

My mind flashed back to Ms Bell's announcement in our assembly a lifetime ago. She had said something about a school pulling out due to an administration error.

"When you already work for the Wilderness Warriors it doesn't take much to send a few … deceptive emails. I got rid of the other school quite easily. Do you really think Linley High is deserving of this kind of invitation?"

He really was a very obnoxious man.

"But that still didn't mean that Lena was going to be one of the students coming, did it?" said Scarlett. "It could have been anyone!"

Dale sighed. "No. It didn't," he said. "And believe me, I had quite an extensive plan to make sure she was chosen. But lo and behold, I didn't need to do a thing. Lena heard where the weekend was taking place and conveniently volunteered herself." He turned to Lena. "Bravo, Lena. Not only are you here, but you then handed the details of the treasure's whereabouts to me on a plate."

My brain was whirring as I thought about the last forty-eight hours.

"You picked up the pieces of paper Lena dropped at the checkpoint yesterday!" I said. I looked at the others. "Do you remember they blew across the grass?"

"Yes! He went and picked them up, and I remember when he walked back he was looking at them," said Scarlett.

Dale did a slow hand-clap.

"Yes, yes, yes. It wasn't exactly hard to work out,

was it?" he snarled. "I saw enough to know you'd probably go off on a detour from the campsite. I just needed you to lead the way."

He tilted his head from side to side and his neck made a horrible clicking sound.

"When I sell that treasure I can go back to the city where there are ceilings and walls and no trees and definitely no sodding kids!"

Scarlett, Lena, Josh and I all looked at each other. What were we going to do? There wasn't time to think as Dale already seemed to have a plan of his own.

"Anyway, this is all getting quite boring. Let's move on to the exciting bit, shall we? The part where *you* go into the mountain and bring out the treasure for me."

"Sure!" said Josh. "We'll get the treasure and find another exit and head the other way. Loser!" Josh made his fingers into an L sign on his forehead. Then Josh seemed to think about it. "There is another way out, isn't there, Lena?" he said.

"I don't know," said Lena.

Dale's sinister smile stayed fixed on his face.

"I've already thought of that possibility," he said. "The thing is, you are going to *want* to come back and give me the treasure in exchange for your … friend." He reached out a hand and grabbed hold of

Lena's shoulder.

"Hey!" said Lena. She tried to shrug him off but he gripped her tightly.

"Get in there and find the treasure and no one will get hurt. OK?" he said. His eyes were wide. I was scared. He looked really quite dangerous.

"B-but why all this?" I said. "Why don't you just go in yourself and get the treasure? We can't stop you. Why do *we* have to go and get it?"

Dale began to laugh. *Really* laugh. He threw his head back, and his mouth mirrored the gaping hole in the mountain and his shoulders shook.

I looked at Josh and Scarlett but they were both as bewildered as I was. Lena was staring at the ground, looking awkward. I got the distinct feeling that there was more to this mountain; than she had told us.

Dale wiped the tears of laughter that had sprung from his eyes.

"Oh, this just gets better and better," he said. "You haven't told them, have you?" He gave Lena a shake and her head jolted backwards.

"No," she said quietly. "But it's not a hundred per cent certain, is it? No one is entirely sure that the rumours are true. I didn't think it was necessary to worry anyone."

My throat was suddenly really dry and I felt a little bit dizzy.

"What didn't you want to worry us about?" I asked.

"Come on, Lena," said Scarlett, also looking concerned. "What is it?"

Lena glanced up at Dale, who was waiting patiently.

"Go on, then, Lena. Tell your unfortunate friends what awaits them inside the *glorious* Fortune Mountain."

Lena looked at Josh, Scarlett and then at me. Her throat rippled as she swallowed.

"Um, well. The thing is," she began. "The thing is … there is a high possibility that the mountain is booby-trapped."

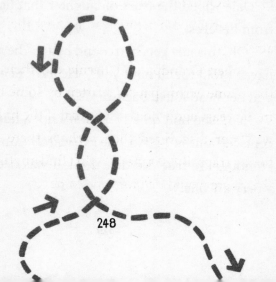

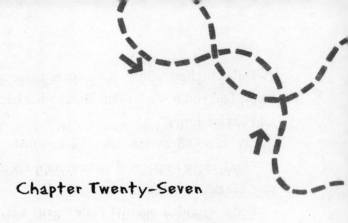

Chapter Twenty-Seven

Entering the Gaping Mouth

"BOOBY-TRAPPED?!" yelled Josh. "What do you mean, BOOBY-TRAPPED?"

Lena rubbed her forehead against the top of her arm.

"When Grandpa and Bernie did their research, they came across papers written by some historians many years ago who thought that if the hiding place was ever discovered then *perhaps* there might be booby traps. But Grandpa didn't find anything to say that there would *definitely* be some."

Dale laughed wildly. "Of course there are booby traps! Did you not tell them about what happened to Old Taylor-Jones?"

"Who is Old Taylor-Jones?" asked Josh.

"And, more importantly, what happened to him?" said Scarlett.

Lena wriggled against Dale's grip again but he held on.

"Old Taylor-Jones was a rival pirate who tried to find the treasure. The story goes that he found the entrance to Walter Morgan's tunnel, went in and was … um … well, he was never seen again."

"Oh, that's just terrific," said Scarlett, letting out one of her famous huffs.

"It's only a story!" said Lena. "It doesn't mean anything bad happened to him."

"Right. Enough time wasting. I've waited long enough for this moment," said Dale. He pointed at me and Josh. "You two. Take your rucksacks off. You won't be needing those."

Lena's and Scarlett's were already on the ground. Josh and I hesitated for a moment, then unhooked ourselves from the straps.

"Now," Dale said, holding out his hand. "The emergency mobile phone. Who has it?"

I wondered if I could somehow deny it, but Dale noticed that everyone was looking at me. I felt my heart pounding. He beckoned with his fingers.

"Come on, come on, I haven't got all day. NOW!" I jumped and then took the plastic bag with the phone inside out of my pocket and slapped it into his palm.

Dale checked it was still off. "I bet you regret not using it now, eh?" he said. Then he lobbed it into the undergrowth.

"Hey. Don't litter! You'll hurt wildlife doing stuff like that," said Josh.

"I'll hurt you if you don't hurry up and get in there," said Dale. He bent down and picked up a glass lantern that he had by his feet. It looked like the kind you might find swinging onboard an old ship.

"You'll need your hands free so no torches. Light this before you go inside. It's going to be very, very dark, and I wouldn't want any of you to come to a sticky end now, would I? Who'd find the treasure for me if that happened?"

He passed the lantern to Scarlett, who took it, glaring at him.

"You really are quite horrible, aren't you?" said Scarlett.

"Ha! I've seen you in action, little girl. You are

quite unpleasant yourself," he snapped back.

A pained look flashed across Scarlett's face. That must have been hard for her to hear. But then Lena tried to wrestle her shoulder free from Dale's grip. "She ISN'T," she yelled. "She's my friend and she is worth TEN of you!"

Dale easily twisted Lena's unharmed arm behind her back. It must have hurt, or maybe it was her injury. Either way, her face turned grey and she looked like she might be sick. With his other hand Dale fished a small box of matches out of his jacket pocket and threw them towards me.

"Catch," he said. I lunged for them but they fell to the ground.

"You'll have to be better than that when you're in there," said Dale. "Even a tiny mistake could end pretty grimly."

I felt my cheeks burning as I picked them up. What on earth were we about to be faced with? And how was I going to cope?

"Time to go now, children. The entrance is right there," said Dale. "And, remember, don't try anything stupid or you *will* regret it. Now, off you trot."

Scarlett, Josh and I hesitated, and I imagined we were all wondering whether we had any options left to not do this, but I couldn't think of one. We made our way to the entrance which was just a few metres away. I looked back at Lena, who gave a shuddered breath and nodded at me, then I turned towards the dark, narrow hole.

"Are we going to fit in there? I mean, it's not much wider than my shoulders," I said.

"I-I don't know," said Scarlett, peering inside. "It looks awfully dark. I wish we had our torches as well."

Josh took the lantern from her hand and opened the little glass door.

"Let's get this alight, shall we?" he said. "I'm sure it won't be that bad once we get inside."

I fumbled with the matchbox and some of the matches fell to the ground.

"COME ON!" hollered Dale. "You're wasting time! The longer you take the more chance your friend here will be in a lot of trouble!"

My hand shook as I tried to get hold of a match. I managed to pick one up but it snapped as I attempted to strike it against the box.

"I can do that, if you like," said Scarlett. I passed the box to her, grateful she was taking over. If it was left to me, all the matches would end up broken.

Scarlett lit the wick inside the lamp and Josh closed the little door.

"Ready?" he said. I nodded.

"Let's do this," said Scarlett.

We turned to the deep crevice.

This was it.

We were going in.

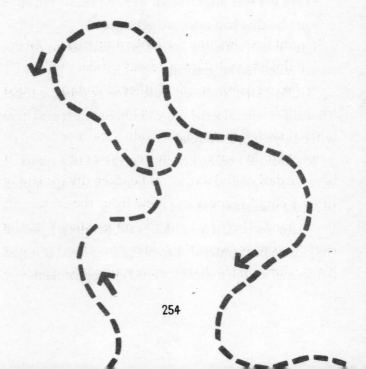

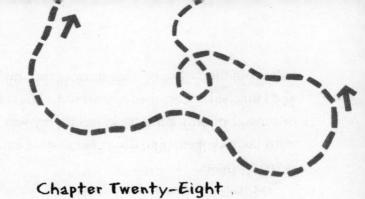

Chapter Twenty-Eight

No Going Back

Josh went first, holding the lantern up high.

"Hello?" he called once he was inside.

Hello... Hello... Hello... the mountain echoed back. He began to edge his way through the gap with Scarlett close behind him. I didn't really want to go last, but I didn't have any choice. As we crept along, it became darker and darker and darker, until the only thing I could see was the glow from the lantern in Josh's hand. There was a dank, rotten smell and the deeper inside we went, the colder it became. I held my hand against the rock wall as we walked to help me to balance in the darkness. It felt slimy against my palm, and I flinched as I brushed against some kind of plant or moss. I put my hand back, feeling my way along until the wall seemed to disappear and we entered a cave-like room.

"Is this it?" said Scarlett. "I can't see a thing! Is the treasure in here?"

"Wait for a moment," said Josh. "We need our eyes to become accustomed to the dark."

The space slowly came into a murky focus. The lamp gave off a yellow glow and there was a tiny sliver of light behind us from the crevice we'd just walked through. In front of us was an archway with a step up that appeared to lead to a corridor. I spotted something written on the wall.

"Hold the lamp up near the top of the arch, Josh," I said. "There's something there."

He held the lantern aloft, lighting up some words that had been scratched into the rock:

BEWARE YE WHO ENTER

I shuddered.

"Well, this isn't creepy in the slightest, is it?" said Scarlett. She was shivering and my legs felt trembly too. Josh took a step towards the archway, and there was a sudden rumbling sound and a rock plummeted from the ceiling, thumping on to the ground right beside him.

Josh froze and slowly turned his head around. "What the—" he began. Behind us there was another rumbling sound but further away. I looked back. The light I had been able to see through the crevice had gone. Dust swirled all around us and Scarlett began to cough. Josh lifted his foot up to step to the side.

"DON'T MOVE, JOSH!" I shouted. "Just stay exactly where you are. You too, Scarlett. It's really important that we all stay absolutely still."

Josh stared down at the large rock beside him, shaking his head. "Well, *I* think we need to get out of here this second before one of us gets killed," he said. "Did you see what nearly landed on my head? We'll just have to sneak out and overpower Dale."

"We can't. The entrance is blocked," I said. "Whatever you triggered made that boulder fall, and it also caused a landslide back there."

I pointed behind us towards another cloud of dust.

"We're trapped?" said Josh.

"We can't be!" said Scarlett. "There *has* to be a

way. We need to check! Vincent, we have to get out of here right now!" She was breathing really quickly and looked like she was getting ready to make a run for it.

"Just don't move, Scarlett!" I said. "I need to think." I suddenly remembered something that I hadn't even thought about in the last forty-eight hours. *Battle Doom*. How would Fabian have coped in this situation?

"Hang on a minute. I remember seeing something like this before!" I said.

"Oh, right, so you've got experience in booby-trapped caves, have you?" said Josh.

"Not exactly. But this reminds me of a level in my computer game."

Josh pulled a face. "Seriously?!"

"Go on, Vincent," said Scarlett. "What do you remember?"

"Fabian – that's the character I'm playing as – well, on one mission he had to walk through the hallway of an old abandoned palace. The hallway floor had these weird patterned tiles, and after I got killed a few times by falling debris, I worked out where it was safe to tread. Josh must have stepped on something to trigger the rock to fall."

I looked at the ground, squinting in the dim

light. I spotted some raised bumps here and there. They looked like little square tiles which had been hidden beneath the dirt. The edge of Josh's trainer was resting on one.

"I know what it is!" I said. "Look at Josh's foot. It's on something. I think he stepped on that, and it set off the falling rock *and* the landslide that's blocked our exit."

Josh looked down at his foot and very carefully eased it off.

Scarlett looked around.

"There are loads of them," she said. "Are you sure about this, Vincent?"

"Yes. I think so," I said. "If we avoid the tiles we should be OK. I'll … um … I guess I'll go first."

I lifted my foot, ready to step on to an area of flat ground in front of me.

"BE CAREFUL!" screeched Scarlett, making me jump so much that I nearly toppled over.

"Scarlett!" I said. "This is really hard for me! Especially in these boots."

"Sorry."

I caught my breath and got ready again. I couldn't let my dyspraxia let me down now. I took a small step forward. Nothing happened. I concentrated hard to make sure I placed my foot in exactly the right spot and moved again.

"It's fine," I said. "Just walk on the flat ground and make your way to the archway really carefully. Hopefully there'll be another exit through there."

Josh swung the lamp close to the ground and we began to walk. I was slow, but I got to the archway and clambered up on to the ledge. Scarlett was biting on her lip as she carefully made her way towards me.

"Be careful, Scarlett, I think there's one just to the left of your right foot," I called out. She froze and took a closer look at the ground, then she moved her foot to a clear space. She reached the ledge and stepped up to join me, followed by Josh.

Josh held up the lantern, and we peered down the dark passageway.

"We're going to walk into another trap, aren't we?" he said.

I looked around the best I could. The ground and the ceiling looked smooth in here. There were no more tiles on the floor, and I couldn't see anything else that might trigger another booby trap.

"I think it's safe," I said. "Come on."

I took three steps along the corridor and was about

to tell the others that we should stick closely together when the ground disappeared from beneath my feet and I felt myself falling.

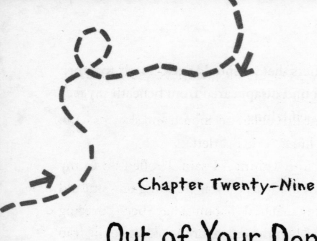

Chapter Twenty-Nine

Out of Your Depth

I landed on my stomach and all of the air shot out of me with an "Oooooofff!"

I knew that I was lying face down but for a moment I was confused about where I was and what had just happened.

"Vincent! Are you OK?" called a voice.

"Talk to us! We can't see you!" said another.

I rolled on to my back and looked up to the top of the deep hole that I had fallen into. There were two faces peering down at me. I put my arm up to block out the glare of a light. Where was I?

"He's alive. Oh, thank goodness," said Scarlett. Josh held up the lamp.

I spat some dirt out of my mouth and slowly sat up.

"Are you hurt?" said Scarlett.

"No. I'm fine, I think," I said. I rolled on to my knees and got to my feet. I was standing on some old brown sacking material that must have been covering the hole. I had literally fallen for the oldest booby trap in the book – the classic 'invisible deep hole'. This was the wildest thing that had ever happened to me and I suddenly found it hilarious. I began to giggle.

"Erm. What's so funny?" called Josh. "Are you all right?"

"Yes, I'm fine!" I said. "It's just … I'm in a hole!" My giggling turned into proper laughter.

"Maybe he's hit his head or something?" said Josh.

"No, I don't think he did," said Scarlett. "I think he might be in shock and it's made him hysterical."

I clutched my stomach as I laughed and soon felt tears rolling down my cheeks. It started to feel a bit painful so I took some deep breaths to try and compose myself.

"How are we going to get him out?" said Scarlett.

"I've *no* idea," said Josh. "Those sides look steep. We need a ladder or a rope."

"But we haven't got either of those. We can't just leave him there."

Hearing them talking like this quickly brought me back to reality. They were right – how *was* I going to get out? I had navigated Fabian out of holes like this many, many times in *Battle Doom*, but in those cases all I needed to do was push the 'Up' button to make him climb. Here I had to actually do it for myself. I ran my hands along the side of the hole, feeling for anything I might be able to grip hold of. My fingers found a tree root just above my head and I pulled myself up, scrabbling my feet as I went. But the root became loose and broke off. I tried again with another one but it instantly snapped. Then I tried to dig my feet into the sides, attempting to make footholds like a ladder, but the soil just crumbled away.

"It's no good!" I called up. "I can't do it!" The tears I'd just had from laughing changed into tears of despair. Was this it? Was I going to be sitting at the bottom of this hole for ever?

I was suddenly plunged into darkness. I looked up. There was no sign of Josh, Scarlett or the lantern.

Where were they? Had they abandoned me? Or had something happened to them too? I could feel panic beginning to grip my chest. What was I going to do? This couldn't be happening!

Just then something flew over the side of the hole.

"Vincent! I found this. Grab on!" Josh's face appeared over the edge. He was holding on to some brown sacking material like the one I had stepped on and fallen through.

"Hold on to the end and we'll pull you out," said Scarlett.

The material was thick and I found it hard to grip.

"It's no good!" I called. "I can't do it!"

"Yes, you can, Vincent!" said Scarlett.

I paused for a moment, taking a deep breath, and tried again. I dug my fingers into the fabric as tightly as I could.

"I'm holding on, but you won't be able to pull me out. I'm too heavy!" I called.

"Wanna bet?" said Josh.

There was a jolt as they tugged on the sheet, and my shoulder bashed against the side. And then, very slowly, I began to rise up, my feet no longer touching the ground. They were doing it! Clumps of soil fell on my head as they hauled me up and then a hand gripped the back of my jacket.

"I've got you," said Josh. I was lifted into the air and landed on solid ground.

"Are you all right, Vincent?" said Scarlett. "I thought you were going to be stuck down there for ever!"

"I'm OK. I'm OK," I said, shaking with relief. "Thank you. Thank you so much."

Josh picked up the lantern and held it aloft. We peered down the passageway.

"I can't see another exit," said Scarlett. "What do we do?"

"We keep going," I said. "There *must* be another way out. There has to be."

I took a couple of steps forward, but Scarlett and Josh didn't move.

"What about the booby traps? We might walk straight into another one," said Josh.

"We'll take it slowly," I said. "If we see anything suspicious then we all need to stop immediately. We have an advantage here – we are expecting something to happen."

"I'm not being funny, Vincent, but you just fell into a massive hole. You didn't expect that to happen, did you?" said Scarlett.

I smiled. "No, I guess not," I said. "But I'm sure I'll spot the next one. Come on. Let's keep moving."

We made our way slowly along the corridor, checking where we were placing our feet with each step. My heart was racing, and I was very, very frightened indeed but I was doing OK.

I thought about Dad's mantra for living a life just a little out of your depth.

"If only you could see me now, Dad," I muttered to myself.

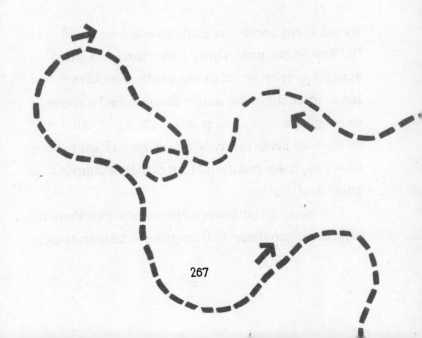

Chapter Thirty

Heading Deeper into the Mountain

As we crept along the dark passageway I felt fear tightening its grip around my throat. I tried to distract myself by thinking of the obstacles I had faced when I played *Battle Doom*. Maybe some of those quests would help me right now? All I had to do was keep my wits about me. If we took it slowly then we might, just might, get through this unscathed.

Josh swung the lantern from left to right as he looked for anything that might potentially trigger some kind of danger. The flame behind the glass window began to flicker.

"Move the lamp slowly, Josh," said Scarlett. "If that flame goes out it's game over."

Josh held the lantern still and the flame settled to a steady burn. We all breathed a sigh of relief and carried on.

Water dripped steadily from the ceiling, and there was a low echoing groaning sound. "What is that horrible noise?" said Scarlett. "It sounds like … wailing."

"I think it's the wind blowing around the mountain," I said, trying to sound braver than I felt. "It's nothing to worry about."

Just then something shot across the ground in front of us.

"AARRGHH!! What was that?" screamed Scarlett. She grabbed my arm and dug her fingernails into my flesh. I caught sight of a long, thick tail.

"It's a rat," I said.

"I HATE RATS!" screamed Scarlett. She began to walk quickly on, but I saw the flicker of something just in front of her foot.

"SCARLETT! STOP!" I shouted. She froze. There was a low, thin cord that stretched across the width of the corridor at ankle level, and it was pressing against the laces of her boot. She looked at me and her head began to tremble.

"W-what is it?" she said. "Is it the rat? Will it bite?"

"No. It's not the rat, but there *is* a tripwire by your feet," I said as calmly as I could. "Just stay still for a second while I have a closer look. Can I take the lantern?" Josh passed it to me.

We could hear the rat scurrying around, and every time there was a noise, Scarlett flinched and her head darted left to right, trying to spot it.

"You've *got* to keep still, Scarlett," said Josh. "The rats won't hurt you, OK? They're more frightened of us than we are of them."

"Them? What do you mean them? I thought there was only one!"

Josh was right. I'd seen at least five. I walked along the length of the tripwire until I reached the wall. There were some holes hollowed out at shoulder height. Pointing out of the holes were lots of razor-sharp silver arrowheads. I walked to the other side and saw there were just as many on this wall.

"What have you found? Tell me!" said Scarlett. I went back to her. She *had* to stay calm or we might end up being showered with deadly-looking arrows.

"Just keep still and everything is going to be all right. OK?" I said. I crouched down and looked at the wire across her foot. It was touching her boot, but it wasn't caught on anything.

"What do I do? Is something going to happen?" said Scarlett. "I'm scared, Vincent." She was trembling and I was worried that she might set the arrows off accidentally.

"You are going to be fine," I said. "Just look straight at me, OK? And listen carefully."

Scarlett fixed her eyes on mine and I smiled to try and relax her.

"That's good," I said. "What I need you to do is to slowly slide your right foot backwards. Don't lift it or try any sudden movements, just move very, very slowly, OK?"

She nodded and then she took a deep breath and began to move her foot back. The cord tensed for a moment, and for a second I thought it had caught on her laces, but then it gently pinged itself free.

"That's it. You've done it!" I said.

Scarlett blew a long breath out of her mouth. "Oh, thank goodness," she said.

I looked over at Josh who was watching, wide-eyed.

"The tripwire is just down here," I said, using the

lamp to light it. "We need to step over it very carefully. I'll go first and check if there's anything suspicious on the other side, and then you can follow."

I stared at the wire.

It was a simple thing to do – to just step over a thin piece of string – but knowing the consequences if one of us caught our foot on it made it quite terrifying. And if anyone was going to make a mess of it, it would be me. I lifted my leg so high that I wobbled on my other one and had to put my arms out to steady myself. Once I got my balance I stepped over, making sure to lift my back leg just as high so I didn't catch it behind me. I made it. I scanned the ground, walls and ceiling using the lamp. I couldn't see anything suspicious.

"It looks safe over here. Just be careful when you step over."

I held the lamp up as Scarlett stepped over. She did it easily but still looked incredibly relieved. For some reason Josh decided to jump over. Scarlett and I gasped as he flew up into the air, then landed on the other side.

"Josh! Did you *have* to do that?" said Scarlett.

"I made it, didn't I?" he said.

Scarlett turned to me and gave me a quick hug.

"Thank you, Vincent. I think you might have just saved my life."

"'S'all right," I said. "Let's just stay vigilant."

We edged along the corridor.

"I wonder what terrifying thing is waiting for us next," said Scarlett softly. "I'm really scared."

I knew what she meant. I was scared too, but we had no option except to press on.

"Come on, let's keep moving," I said.

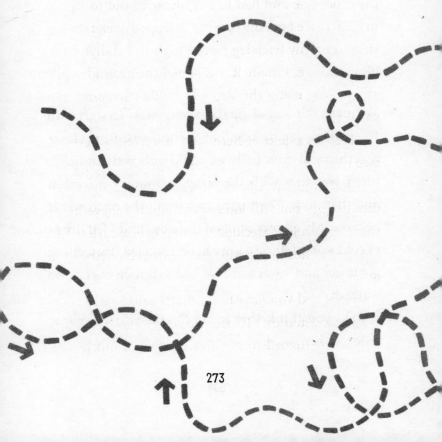

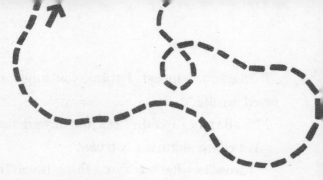

Chapter Thirty-One

Treasure Island

We made our way along the passageway. To start with we walked side by side, but the walls became closer together and eventually we could only walk in single file. I was first with the lamp, followed by Scarlett and then Josh. The further we went, the narrower it became. My elbows scraped the sides and I felt drops of cold water falling on my head and face. The ceiling got lower and lower until we had to hunch over as we walked.

"Do you think this is safe?" said Scarlett, panic rising in her voice.

"Maybe we should turn back and look for another way?" said Josh, who also sounded frightened. "It might be another trap and we'll end up getting squashed like sardines in a can!"

I was wondering the same thing when the passageway began to widen again.

"I don't think it's a trap," I said. "I can see something. We're nearly at the end of the corridor."

The passageway widened enough for us to stand side by side again, and I held the lantern up and squinted into the gloom. This was a cavernous space. When I looked up I couldn't see the ceiling. The walls trickled with water, and the wailing noise, which I was still hoping was just the wind, echoed all around us.

I heard Scarlett take a deep breath. "I dread to think what's coming for us in here," she said.

But Josh laughed. "There's nothing coming next," he said. "Look! It's the treasure!"

In the centre of the room was a large stone table. Spread across the table was a kaleidoscope of jewels and gems, gold and silver.

"Oh, wow! WOW!" said Scarlett. "Look at it all! It's so beautiful."

We walked a little closer, mesmerized by the

incredible spread in front of us. But then I noticed something.

"Hang on. We can't go any further," I said. A deep ditch circled the table of jewels in the centre of the cave like a moat which was as wide as the length of our minibus. I peered down into the ditch. Glinting at me were hundreds and hundreds of sharp, pointed cutlasses and swords. Their handles had been buried so that the blades pointed upright.

"Wow. He really didn't want anyone to get to his treasure, did he?" said Josh, taking a look.

"It's like he's created his very own treasure island," I said.

Scarlett snorted. "Yeah, I guess he has," she said. "How do we get across?"

Josh began to look around.

"Be careful, Josh," I said.

He walked to a dark corner by the cave wall and began to drag something out from the shadows. It was a long piece of flat wood.

"We can use this," he said. "There's a whole pile of them over there. I think it'll reach." He went to the edge of the moat and stood the wood up on its end, then let it drop. The top end of the wood landed on the other side with a deep thud that reverberated around the cave. Josh had made a bridge for us to walk across.

"Sorted!" said Josh. "Shall we go?"

"What do you think, Vincent?" said Scarlett.

I stared at the table of incredible jewels and then down into the moat, at the shiny cutlasses pointing upwards, protecting the treasure. In amongst the sharp blades were pieces of wood similar in colour to the one Josh had found. It was like someone had tried this before. And failed.

"I don't know," I said. "Just give me a second."

"What do you mean?" said Josh. "Everything is right there, ready for the taking. Come on! Let's go fill our pockets."

He was about to go when something clicked in my mind. Josh was about to make a *terrible* mistake.

"Wait!" I called. "It's another trap! Walter wants us to walk the plank!"

But Josh had already stepped on to the wood. Something gave way on the other side of the moat and the plank began to fall. And then Josh disappeared, right in front of our eyes.

Chapter Thirty-Two

Whatever You Do, Don't Let Go

"JOSH!" Scarlett and I screamed in unison. We both ran to the edge and dropped on to our stomachs.

"I'm all right!" he cried. He was hanging from a tree root just over the lip of the ditch. His legs dangled down, a boot scraping the top of a particularly vicious-looking cutlass. The plank he'd stepped on was now in chunks scattered around the ditch floor, sliced like cheese by the collection of blades.

Josh reached a hand towards us, and Scarlett and

I grabbed hold of his arm, pulling him to safety. He sat on the ground, shaking.

"Walking the plank, eh?" he said and then he yelled into the cave. "Not exactly an original one there, Walter! We're not giving up, you know!"

I stood up and looked over at the stone table again. There *must* be a safe way! After all, Walter must have got back across to have escaped the mountain. In *Battle Doom*, I sometimes stumbled across little secrets that would help Fabian to complete a task, like a small lever that opened a trapdoor or a hidden ladder to help him explore. It was all a matter of looking closely. I took a slow walk around the edge of the cave, feeling the walls for any concealed mechanisms or secret objects that might be of use. When I was about to give up, my hand brushed against a rough piece of rope, tucked behind a metal hook. I took the rope out. It was fixed to the ceiling right above the table of treasures. I gave it a tug. It felt strong and secure.

"This is it," I said. "This is the way to get across. Walter left that rope hidden. I reckon he used it to swing across and back again when he was setting all of this up."

"And what if you're wrong?" said Josh. "What if it's just another trap?"

"I don't think it is. You said there were a few planks over there, right? I believe they were deliberately left there for people to use."

"And to plummet on to the swords!" said Josh, his voice trembling.

"This rope, however, was hidden, like he didn't want anyone to find it."

Scarlett nodded. "Makes sense," she said. "Who is going to go first?"

I was beginning to feel quite sick. I remembered that awful party of Ewan's. The one where I couldn't swing across the foam pit on a rope. I'd been so embarrassed that day. But here there was more at stake than being humiliated. I glanced at the moat of shiny blades and shuddered.

"I'll go first," said Josh.

He twisted his arm tightly around the rope and took the lantern in his other hand. With one deft swoop he was across. He made it look so easy.

"Nice one, Josh!" said Scarlett. "Swing the rope back and I'll go next. I want to get it over with."

She caught the rope from Josh and held it tight. Taking a few steps back she ran and then launched herself across, landing safely next to Josh. She turned, a look of relief on her face.

"You'll be fine, Vincent," she called. "It's easy!"

She swung the rope back to me, but I missed it and it headed back to the island. Scarlett got hold of it again.

"Don't worry. You can do this. Ready?" she said. I nodded, not feeling confident in the slightest. This time the rope flew past me, but I caught it on its way back.

"Great! Make sure you get a good run-up," said Josh. "And whatever you do, don't let go!"

I was trembling as I took a few steps back from the edge. I twisted my right hand around the rope and took a firm grip with my left. I suddenly wished Ewan was here. It dawned on me how much I missed not living with my big brother. I was pretty sure he had no idea how much. If I got out of this mountain in one piece, I decided I would make sure I told him.

"Come on, Vincent!" called Scarlett.

I took a long, deep breath, took another two steps back, ran to the edge and launched myself into the air. I felt my body fly and stretched my legs forward.

"That's it! Let go!" shouted Josh. But I couldn't do it. I just couldn't let go. I'd spent my life failing at things like this. Why was this going to be any different? The rope took me right back to where I'd started and this time I did let go, falling into a heap by the very edge of the pit. I panted, my heart racing as I looked over the side at the razor-sharp swords.

The rope had swung back towards Josh and he'd grabbed it.

"You were so close," he said. "Try again!"

I got up and Josh sent the rope back to me. It hit me in the cheek, and I fumbled and caught it.

"You can definitely do this! OK, Vincent?" said Scarlett.

I nodded, but I felt like I was drowning in fear. I held on to the rope and moved backwards again. This was it. There was no going back now.

"You have got this," I whispered to myself. And then I ran.

This time I looked down. I watched the sea of blades shimmering beneath me and then I saw solid ground. I let go. For a moment, I thought I'd judged it wrong and I was actually over the ditch. I braced myself but then my knees hit the cave floor.

"You did it!" yelled Scarlett.

My arms and legs were trembling. "Did I?" I said.

"Well done, Vincent," said Josh, patting me on the shoulder. I got up and looked back across the moat. The rope was dangling beside me. I *had* done it!

"Come on, let's take a look at this treasure, shall we?" said Scarlett.

The amount of gems, gold and silver was breathtaking. Even in the darkness, the whole table seemed to sparkle. But something still didn't feel right. Could there be one last trap? Walter's final attempt at protecting his precious hoard? Surely the treasure would be hidden away in a locked chest or something? Not on display to be taken. Yes, we had to find a safe way across the pit of cutlasses, but if this was *Battle Doom* there would definitely be a final task.

"Whoa, look at the size of this one!" said Josh. He reached for a red stone that was larger than a tennis ball.

"Wait a second!" I cried. "Don't touch anything. Not yet."

"But the treasure is right here! Look, you can see it for yourself. Jewels, gold, silver. Let's take as much as we can carry."

He held his hand out again.

"NO!" I yelled. Scarlett and Josh looked at me, confused. "Games *never* end this way. It's too easy! It doesn't make sense that you can just take the treasure like this. This isn't over yet. I need a moment to figure out what we should do."

On the ground beside the table was a mound of tatty-looking clothing.

"Hang on. There's something down here," I said. I spotted a dark navy jacket and a brown three-peaked hat with a long red feather tucked into it. Using my foot, I lifted the hat up and flinched when I saw what was underneath. It was a bright white skull. The empty eye sockets stared back at me, and the few yellow teeth that remained appeared to be grinning.

"I think I've found what happened to Old Taylor-Jones," I said quietly. "He must have got this far too. There was a broken plank in the ditch, but he must have got lucky and managed to scramble up on to this side."

Scarlett and Josh came to take a look.

"Not so lucky now, though, I guess," said Josh, grimacing.

I couldn't believe this was actually happening. It wasn't so long ago when Lena had told us about this place, and we were all thinking it was just a made-up story. But here was the body of a man. A man who had also tried to find the treasure.

"What happened to him, do you think?" said Scarlett.

"I don't know," I said. "I can't see any obvious

injuries or … hang on. It looks like he was holding something." Poking out of a jacket sleeve was a bony hand with an object in it. I looked around the floor and picked up a small stick, which I hooked on the sleeve and pulled it away. The hand snapped off at the wrist.

"Argh!" I said, jumping away.

"Oh, man," said Josh. "That is gross!"

Something rolled out from between the skeleton's fingers and on to the dirt. I kneeled down, taking the lamp and holding it a little closer. It was a green jewel the size of a lemon.

"He must have taken it from the table," I said.

"It's huge! Can you imagine how much that is worth?" said Scarlett.

"It might be millions," said Josh. I could tell he was itching to pick it up.

"Maybe," I said. "But until we can work out what happened to Old Taylor-Jones we shouldn't touch a thing." We went back to the table. The jewels glinted in the lamplight as I hovered the lantern closer.

"There's a pot of gold and a pot of silver," said Josh.

"Those are pieces of eight, I reckon," I said.

"Really?" said Josh. "I thought that was just made up for kids' stories!"

"No, they were Spanish coins," I said. "Lena would have loved to see all of this."

"Oh, look! There's a note!" said Scarlett.

Tucked beside an ornate golden jug was a brown piece of paper with faded writing on it. I pulled the sleeve down on my jacket and covered my hand to pick it up. I didn't trust anything in here.

"It's from Walter Morgan," I said. "His handwriting is really bad. But I think it says:

> *Ye got this far and ye didn't die*
> *But I's afraid, your ending is nigh.*
> *My treasures are here, just one you can take.*
> *But which is real and which is a fake?*
> *Choose wisely now, and try to be smart*
> *Or poison will stop ye right in ye heart.*
> *Walter Morgan Esq"*

I folded the note and put it into my pocket.

"Is he saying that if we pick up the wrong thing, we'll … die?" asked Josh.

"Yes," I said.

"That's what happened to Old Taylor-Jones. He chose the wrong thing!" said Scarlett. "It must have been coated in something that poisoned him. It's a good job Vincent stopped you picking anything up, Josh."

Josh blinked back at her. He looked shocked.

This challenge was quite mind-blowing and not like anything I'd faced in *Battle Doom*. There were hundreds of objects in front of us, and I wasn't sure if we'd be able to go any further. But then going back was not an option for us either.

"What do we do, Vincent?" said Josh. "Have you got any ideas?"

Only one piece of treasure was genuine and safe for us to pick up. But which one could it be?

"We choose very carefully indeed," I said.

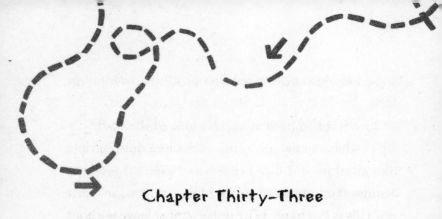

Chapter Thirty-Three

What to Choose...?

"OK," said Josh, rubbing his chin. "Well, it must be that one. Look at the size of it!" He pointed again to the huge ruby-like stone that was balancing on top of a wooden block. "It's the biggest and it must be the most valuable. What do you think?"

"Just because it's large, doesn't mean it's genuine *or* worth the most," I said.

"Well, it looks like a winner to me," said Jake, eyeing the ruby. "I vote for that one."

I scoured the items. There was a delicate-looking tiara made of thin gold with pink-coloured stones inserted into the swirls and a long necklace with a giant pearl the size of a small egg dangling from the middle. There was also a silver box which had little flowers hammered all over it. It looked quite simple compared to the other items so were we supposed to dismiss it on purpose?

"This is too hard. Why don't we just leave without taking anything?" said Scarlett. "Dale can come in here and choose something himself as far as I'm concerned!"

"Good idea, but we can't get out, remember?" said Josh. "We're trapped in here."

I scratched my cheek. "If we choose the right thing it might help us to find an exit. I think Walter Morgan has constructed this like some silly game thinking he can outsmart us. If we pick the right object, then we've won."

I walked up and down beside the table and studied everything closely. I had found four valuable gems in *Battle Doom*. Might that help me find the right thing here as well? First I'd found the ruby. In the game there was a side story about a man who had stolen the gem from a prince as he was desperate to feed his family. The man buried it in his garden, intending to chip bits off it when he needed it. I'd dug up the stone and stolen it back. I'd felt a bit bad about it at the time, but the ruby's rightful place was in the Scorpion Sword. The sapphire took me weeks to find, but eventually I spotted that it had been disguised as an eyeball in a stone statue of a panther which was guarding a knight's tomb. I'd walked past it so many times without noticing. The amethyst wasn't hard to find but it was hard to reach. Within the story I had discovered that it had been picked out of the sword by an eagle many years ago and was hidden in his nest on top of a tall tower. Climbing to the top of the tower was the hardest part for that one – I kept falling off and having to restart the level.

"Maybe we could use a piece of clothing to pick something up and see what happens? So it's not touching our skin, I mean," said Scarlett.

I had already thought of that.

"I wouldn't want to risk it. The poison might be so deadly it could seep through. Or maybe picking the wrong thing might trigger another kind of deadly booby trap," I said.

Just then, my eyes focused on a grubby object, about the size of my palm. It was balancing on top of a silver stand.

"Hang on," I said. "That looks weirdly familiar."

I pointed and Scarlett and Josh peered at it closely.

"It looks like a lump of old glass to me," said Scarlett. "That can't be valuable."

I held the lamp closer. The glass had a yellow tinge to it.

"It's not even carved nicely or anything," said Josh. "Nah. It can't be that."

But the yellowing stone reminded me of something. It reminded me of the travelling hawker in *Battle Doom*. He had been insistent on trying to sell me something that looked very similar to this – an old yellowing stone that matched the colour of his teeth. What if it wasn't just a stone? What if it was important? And he'd said those strange words when he'd grabbed on to Fabian's arm the night before I left for the weekend.

"I heard something recently," I said. My mind was racing as I tried to recall what the man had said to me. "It was something like, 'beauty can be found in the misunderstood or the underestimated', or something like that."

I turned to face Scarlett and Josh. They looked puzzled.

"I know it sounds silly but in my game there's this travelling salesman who keeps trying to sell me a dirty lump of stone. And it looks exactly like that!" I pointed at the rock. "In the quest I've been trying to find the final precious gem to complete the game. And now I've realized that's what the travelling hawker had all along. He was trying to sell me a rough diamond!"

"A what?" said Josh.

"It's a raw diamond before it's been cut and polished," said Scarlett. "They don't come out of the ground all neat and sparkly like they look in rings and stuff."

"Oh, right," said Josh.

"I bet Walter Morgan thought that anyone who gets this far and sees all these sparkling gems would just ignore this dull-looking one. *That's* why he put it here with the others. He thinks he can beat us."

I grinned.

"OK," said Josh, "let's say that lump there *is* the treasure. What do we do now? What if you're wrong? What was is that Walter said? *Poison will stop ye right in the heart.*"

I looked at the rough diamond.

"There's no other choice," I said. "I have to try."

I reached out my hand and it trembled in front of the stone.

"Vincent?" said Scarlett. "Are you sure you know what you're doing?"

I looked at her and took a deep breath.

"I think so," I said. In my head I counted to three, and then I grabbed the stone and lifted it off its stand.

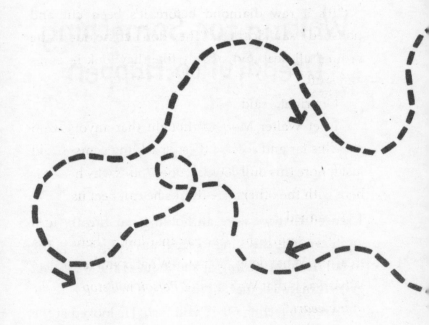

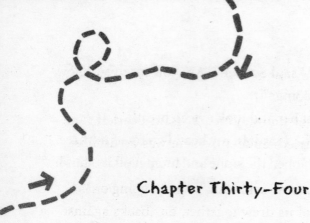

Chapter Thirty-Four

Waiting for Something Dreadful to Happen

I sensed that we were all holding our breath. Josh spun around, checking to see if anything was going to fall from the ceiling or shoot out of the walls. But everything was quiet.

"Are you feeling OK?" said Josh. He looked at the diamond in my bare hand.

"You don't feel sick or anything, do you?" said Scarlett. "Or dizzy?"

I thought about it.

"No," I said. "I guess if it is poisoned I'll know about it soon. Won't I?"

"I … I don't know, Vincent," said Scarlett. She looked so worried. Suddenly there was a rumbling noise.

"W-what's that?" said Josh. "What's going on?"

The three of us drew together, our backs against each other as we faced outwards, waiting for something awful to appear. Then Scarlett pointed behind the table of gems.

"Look! Daylight!" she said.

At the far end of the cavern was a thin strip of light.

"It's an opening," I said. "I feel fine so it must be OK. Come on!"

I shoved the stone into my pocket and grabbed the rope. I had to do it again! This time I swung across but only just reached the edge.

"That was close!" yelled Scarlett. They both followed me, and then we let go of the rope so it swung back to the island. We'd got what we needed now.

The light was coming from a passageway at the back of the cavern. We made our way through. It was really tight in places, and at one point I thought we might actually get stuck, but eventually I felt a slight breeze on my face and leaves brushing against the top of my head. The exit was blocked by some branches, and I twisted them to one side before tumbling out on to a patch of soft green grass. I lay on my back and looked up at the blue sky between the dappled leaves of a tree.

"Ah!" I said. "Fresh air!" I breathed in. It smelled so sweet after the stuffy, dusty mountain. Scarlett and Josh sat down beside me.

"I never thought I'd be so pleased to be in the outdoors," said Scarlett. "Hello, grass! Hello, trees! It's so nice to see you." Josh and I laughed. Scarlett looked so different to how she was at the beginning of the trip. There were smudges of dirt across her cheeks and her shiny brown hair was tangled and messy. I imagined I probably looked different too and I smiled to myself. But then I remembered this still wasn't over. We had to get our friend back.

"Which way are Dale and Lena?" I said. I'd lost all sense of direction after being in the dark for so long.

Josh looked around us. "They'll be over that way." He pointed through the trees. "We need to walk around the base of the mountain and we'll reach them eventually."

"I hope Lena's OK," said Scarlett. "It feels like we've been gone for ages."

"What are we going to do when we get there?" I said. "Just hand the diamond over to Dale?"

"I guess," said Josh. "He won't let Lena go if we don't."

"It doesn't seem fair," I said. "We went through so much to get this." I held the rough diamond up in the sunlight. Out here I could see more clearly that it wasn't just a dull stone. It glimmered in the light, giving hints of its potential to be a beautiful jewel once it had been cut and polished.

"Give the diamond to me," said Scarlett. "I've got an idea."

She held out her hand, and I placed the stone in her palm.

"Just follow me and do what I say, OK? Let's be as quiet as possible."

I frowned at Josh. What was going on? We began to walk through the undergrowth with Scarlett leading the way. We made our way through more scratchy plants, and before long we spotted the hooked rock nose on the side of the mountain and we crouched in a bush. Scarlett pointed a finger towards the clearing.

"They're over there," she mouthed. Dale was pacing back and forth with his hands on his hips, while Lena was sitting on the ground, propped against a tree. She looked pale and she was biting her lip like she was in a lot of pain.

"Let's do this!" said Scarlett. And before we had a chance to ask what 'this' was, she burst through the branches with us following.

"Hey!" she yelled.

Dale spun round. "At last! What took you so long?"

Scarlett held the diamond up. "Is this what you wanted?"

He scowled at the rock. "That?!" he exclaimed. "Do you think I'm a fool or something?"

"Well, it had crossed our minds, actually," said Josh. Dale stormed over to us, and we all took a step back.

"I asked for the treasure. Not a piece of rubbish!" he spat. "Where is it? You've hidden it, haven't you?" Behind his shoulder, I could see that Lena was staring at the diamond in Scarlett's hand. I watched as a small smile spread across her face. She must have worked out what it was.

"It is the treasure," said Lena, wincing in pain. "But if you were a proper investigator you would know that, wouldn't you?"

Dale looked back at her, then at Scarlett.

"It's a rough diamond, you loser!" yelled Scarlett.

She held it up in her fist. Dale's wide eyes blinked as he stared at it, and then he reached out a hand.

"Hand it over then," he said.

Scarlett lifted the diamond to shoulder height. "If you want it so much, go and get it!" she said and then she threw it into the bushes.

Dale looked close to erupting into a human volcano.

"What did you do that for?" He ran over to the dense undergrowth and crouched down to try and find the diamond. Scarlett then ran full pelt towards him, shoving him straight into a patch of stinging nettles.

"Arrgh!" he cried.

Scarlett quickly kneeled on top of him as he lay there, sprawled on the ground.

"Josh!" she called. "Come and help me!"

Josh sprinted over and sat on the back of Dale's legs.

"Get off me!" Dale yelled. But Josh was tall and stronger than he looked, and Dale couldn't move with the two of them sitting on him.

"Vincent. Grab a first-aid kit and bring over the rolls of bandages!" said Scarlett. I ran to my rucksack and took mine out.

"Are you OK, Lena?" I asked. She nodded but she

didn't look good to me.

Scarlett tied Dale's wrists together and then his ankles and, with Josh's help, they pulled him out of the nettles.

"You won't get away with this!" said Dale. "You are making a BIG mistake!"

Josh carefully picked his way around the nettles and came out a few seconds later.

"Got it!" he said, holding the diamond aloft.

I headed into the undergrowth where Dale had thrown the emergency phone earlier.

"I was so worried about you guys!" called Lena. "How was it? Was it really scary? You've got to tell me *everything*!"

Dale was still grunting and yelling out, but eventually I found the phone and broke the seal on the bag. I turned it on and called Ms Bell.

"VINCENT! Oh my goodness!" she gasped. "Are you OK? Where are you? We've been so worried!"

"We're all fine, Ms Bell. Although Lena has hurt her wrist. We think it might be broken. We had a run-in with Dale and he's currently, um, tied up here with us. He held Lena hostage."

"THEY'RE LYING!" yelled Dale, with his cheek against the mud. I ignored him.

"Dale?" she said. "Are you sure? We thought he was out searching for you."

"We can tell you all about it when you get here," I said. "It's a long story."

"OK, Vincent," she said, sounding quite bewildered. "Now, where are you?"

I described the overhanging rock and Ms Bell said she knew exactly where we were as she'd been climbing here before.

"We'll be with you as soon as we can. Just hang in there," she said. I rang off.

"Here you are, Lena," said Josh. "This belongs to you. I think you are now officially rich!"

He handed the rough diamond to Lena, who held it up with her uninjured hand.

"It is quite beautiful," she said. "But it's not mine. It'll be declared as treasure and go to a museum."

"Really?" said Josh. "You're not keeping it to sell?"

Lena shook her head. "Even if I could, I wouldn't want to. None of this was about the money. I just wanted to prove that Grandpa wasn't a silly old man. And because of all of you I can tell everyone that he was a treasure hunter. And a successful one at that."

"Ha! That is ridiculous," said Dale. "You're

pathetic. Just like your grandpa!"

"I think you'll find that you're the one lying flat on your face, tied up with bandages and *we* have the diamond," said Josh. "Who's the pathetic one again?"

Dale thrashed about in the dirt and then stopped when he realized he wasn't getting anywhere.

Lena got up and we moved away from Dale's moaning and groaning and leaned against a rock.

"What was it like in the mountain?" said Lena. "I wish I could have gone inside."

"It was AWFUL," said Scarlett, sipping from her bottle. "It was really scary and dark and cold. You would have loved it!"

Lena smiled. We told her about the rock falling at the start which nearly hit Josh, then me falling into the hole and the tripwire on Scarlett's foot almost setting off the arrows. Josh explained how he had accidentally walked the plank and that we had swung on a rope across a pit of swords to choose from a huge pile of treasure.

"Oh, and we found a skeleton which we think must be Old Taylor-Jones," said Scarlett. "He failed at the last stage."

"So that story was true!" said Lena. "Poor guy."

"You should have seen the last cave, Lena! There was so much gold and silver and gems. I would have just grabbed them all, but Vincent here was amazing and knew there was one final test," said Josh.

"There was a note from Walter, so I knew we had to choose one item carefully," I said.

Lena's eyes were wide open. "He left a note?"

I took the folded piece of paper out of my pocket. It seemed very thin and fragile in the sunlight.

"Yep. Here you go." Lena opened the note and read it. "This is incredible," she said, tears in her eyes. "This is actually Walter's handwriting! Wow. Grandpa would have loved this."

"Do you think any of the other things on the table were actually valuable or do you think they were fake?" said Scarlett.

Lena frowned. "I don't know. The note says they're fake. I guess this site is a place of historical interest now. A team of archaeologists will want to check it all out once it's made safe, and they'll find out more."

"And what about Old Taylor-Jones?" I said. "What will happen to him?"

"I guess the police will need to check that out and then he'll get a proper burial," said Lena. She was shivering so Scarlett got a foil blanket from her first-aid kit and wrapped it around her shoulders.

We heard the distant thud of a helicopter heading

our way. Scarlett turned to the three of us.

"Before everyone gets here and things get hectic. Can I just say … you lot are all right, you know? It's been quite a weekend," she said.

"Yeah, I agree," said Josh. "You guys are the best."

Lena had a tear rolling down her cheek and wiped it away as she nodded. I think she was in too much pain to speak. I had a big lump in my throat. It had been the most incredible couple of days, and I was struggling to find the right words to tell the others what I was feeling. And then I knew what I wanted to say.

"I think these have probably been the best three days of my life," I said.

Josh nodded and Scarlett reached out and patted me on my leg.

"Yep," said Josh.

"Agreed," said Scarlett.

"Me too," said Lena.

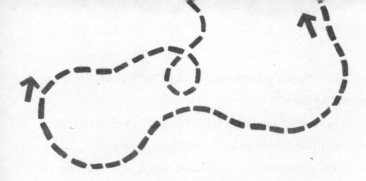

Chapter Thirty-Five

Reunited

When the helicopter was overhead, Scarlett, Josh and I stood up and waved as it hovered over the tops of the trees. They must have spotted us and alerted others on the ground to our exact position as within seconds, three jeeps hurtled through the trees and skidded to a stop just beside our rucksacks. Carmen from the Wilderness Warriors team, Ms Bell and Mr Hearn jumped out of one of the jeeps, a paramedic and two police officers from another, and a man and a woman in red search-and-rescue jackets from the last. The helicopter tilted in the air and flew away.

"Oh, thank goodness you're OK!" said Ms Bell, hurrying over.

"You really gave us a fright there!" said Mr Hearn.

"Is anyone hurt at all?" said the paramedic.

"Can you check Lena?" said Scarlett. "The rest of us are OK but she's hurt her arm. I tried to bandage it the best I could."

The paramedic went to Lena and inspected her wrist. Lena's fingers looked very swollen and a bit blue-ish, which I guessed wasn't a good sign.

"Hello, Lena. Everything is going to be all right. We'll get you to the hospital and get this X-rayed, and in the meantime I'll give you something for the pain," said the paramedic. As she went through her kit bag she looked up at Scarlett. "That's some excellent first-aid work. Well done."

Scarlett blushed. The search-and-rescue team checked in with me, Josh and Scarlett. Then they noticed Dale lying on the floor.

"Dale?" said Carmen, spotting her colleague. "What's going on?"

"These kids tied me up and threatened me!" he yelled, struggling against the bandages. "I tried to call you, but … but I couldn't!"

"He's lying!" said Scarlett.

"He held Lena captive and made us go into the mountain and it was booby-trapped," I said. I turned to Carmen. "He's not the nice guy you think he is. He only worked for you to be close to Fortune Mountain so he could try and find some lost treasure."

"I think we need to have a chat, sir," said one of the police officers. She took some handcuffs from her belt and turned to us. "We'll need to speak to you four, but we'll do that back at the camp. My colleagues are on their way. She walked towards Dale. "So, sir, can you explain what's been going on here and why you didn't alert the authorities that you'd found the missing party?"

While Dale rambled on about how innocent he was, Mr Hearn and Ms Bell focused on us.

"What on earth were you thinking?" said Mr Hearn.

"We are very, very pleased to see you, but you have some explaining to do, not only to us but to your families as well," said Ms Bell.

"Oh, what?" said Josh, rolling his eyes. "My dad is going to be *so* angry."

"He'll be too relieved to see you to be angry," said Mr Hearn. "As will all of your families."

"Are you saying that our parents are *here*?" said

Scarlett. She looked really worried.

"Yes. They arrived a couple of hours ago," said Ms Bell.

"And mine too?" I said.

"Yes, Vincent. Your mum, dad and your brother travelled here late last night after we'd called them to say you were missing," said Ms Bell. "You'll see them shortly." I felt sick thinking how worried they must have been. It was at that moment that Ms Bell spotted what Lena was holding in her hand.

"Oh my goodness," she said. "Is that… Is that a … diamond?!"

"Yes," said Lena. "It's Walter Morgan's treasure."

"Walter Morgan, the pirate from the seventeenth century?" said Mr Hearn. His eyes were twinkling like the diamond. "How on earth did you find that?"

The four of us looked at each other.

"It's a very long story," I said.

"Well, you can explain it all on the way back to the camp," said Carmen. "Your families are very keen to see you so I think we should get moving. You must be hungry and thirsty too, I'm guessing?"

"Oh, yes!" said Josh.

As we made our way to the jeeps, Dale started yelling again.

"Get your hands off me!" he yelled. "They're little liars and thieves!" The police officer had put the handcuffs on him and was holding his cuffed hands at his back. Dale spotted us climbing into the jeeps.

"That diamond isn't yours, you know! You are stealing it! It's THEFT!"

His shouts faded away as we drove off.

Lena went back with the paramedics, and the other three of us explained to our teachers about how Lena was on a secret mission to try and find Walter Morgan's lost treasure in memory of her grandpa. And how her grandpa used to be in partnership with Dale's father.

"It sounds like Dale has issues to work through," said Ms Bell.

"Will he be in a lot of trouble?" said Scarlett.

"He'll lose his job, for sure. And then there's the fact that he didn't tell us he'd found you, and he held Lena against her will. So, yes. I think he's in a whole heap of trouble," said Mr Hearn.

We got back to the camp we had set off from two days ago. Mr Hearn parked near the Wilderness Warriors office and I spotted an ambulance, presumably to take Lena to hospital.

"Look. There are the other teams," said Josh. Under the gazebo was a crowd of muddy-looking people. Some were standing up but a lot of them were sitting on the ground looking pretty exhausted. In amongst them I spotted the yellow beanie hat wearers of Royal Crescent High standing with their teacher, Mr Mac. They all had medals around their necks.

"I'm guessing they won then?" I asked Ms Bell.

"Yep. But not everyone finished," she said. "One team lost their way completely and ended up near a dual carriageway so they had to get picked up. And another used the phone to say they'd had enough so they were disqualified."

We probably wouldn't have been the losers after all, then, but I realized that I didn't care about that any more. I scanned the faces in the crowd but couldn't spot my family. Lena was there and her parents appeared from the throng of people and hurried over.

"Lena! Are you OK? What happened to you?" said her mum, throwing her arms around her. Lena flinched as her mum accidentally squashed her wrist.

"Ow! I'm fine, Mum," said Lena.

Lena's dad rubbed her back.

"We are so pleased you are all right," he said. He

looked very tearful. "But what were you thinking, going off like that?"

Lena's head dropped.

"I'm sorry. I just wanted to prove that Grandpa knew what he was talking about. He was so certain there was treasure to be found. And he was right. Look!"

Lena revealed the treasure from her pocket.

"It's a rough diamond," she said. Her parents looked at each other, open-mouthed.

"I see," said her mum. "So all those things Dad used to talk about. They were ... true? The pirate and the hidden cave?"

Lena nodded. "He *knew* there was treasure hidden in that mountain and now I ... I mean, *we* have shown that he was right all along."

Lena's mum smiled. "He would be so proud of you, Lena," she said.

"Although it doesn't excuse going off on an adventure like that," said her dad. "Anything could have happened."

"What's that you've got there, then?" hollered Dougie from Royal Crescent High. He was looking at the diamond in Lena's hand. Mr Hearn and Ms Bell appeared beside us with our rucksacks.

"Ms Bell?" said Mr Mac. "Your team is aware that this wasn't supposed to be a litter pick, weren't they? Is that what took them so long?" Dougie and the rest of his team sniggered.

Ms Bell put her hands on her hips.

"*That* is not litter, Mr MacKenzie. And considering that you are a chemistry teacher, I am very surprised that you haven't recognized exactly what it is."

Mr Mac's grin dropped and he squinted as Lena held it up. As if it knew it was being studied it began to twinkle ever so slightly in the sunlight.

"It's an uncut diamond," said Ms Bell. "And a rather large one at that. I'd estimate it's probably worth tens of thousands of pounds."

Dougie's eyebrows shot up so high they disappeared into his beanie.

Mr Mac cleared his throat. "I see," he said. "That is quite a sum!"

"Not that money was the goal here, of course," continued Ms Bell. "Lena's quest was all about finding the truth. Not financial gain."

I noticed Mr Hearn squeeze her arm, and Ms Bell turned around and smiled at him.

"Right, Lena. We need to get you off to hospital now," said the paramedic.

"But before you go I'm afraid I'm going to have to take that piece of treasure off of you now," said an approaching police officer. "We'll keep it safe and get it looked at by an expert."

Lena nodded and gave the diamond one last look before handing it over.

"We'll see you soon, Lena," said Scarlett.

"Yeah, get fixed quickly!" said Josh.

"Take care, Lena," I said.

Then the paramedic ushered her and her parents to the waiting ambulance.

I scanned the crowd again for my family, and suddenly an arm swooped over my shoulder. I looked up and saw Ewan.

"Been on an adventure, have we?" he said, grinning.

"Something like that," I said. He put his arms around me, and over his shoulder I saw Mum and Dad hurrying towards us. A moment later I had the three of them enveloping me into the best hug I'd ever had.

"Are you OK?" said Dad, letting me go. "You're not hurt, are you?"

"I'm fine," I said.

Mum held me out in front of her. She picked a few

bits of debris out of my hair.

"We were *so* worried about you, Vincent. How did you cope out on your own in the wilderness like that? You must have hated it!"

I crinkled up my nose. They didn't know the half of it yet or anything about what we'd had to face in the mountain.

"You know what, Mum?" I said, smiling. "It was actually all right."

Mum frowned and looked at Dad, who seemed just as puzzled.

I spotted Josh being squeezed by his dad, who appeared to have tears rolling down his face. Scarlett was with her parents as well, and her mum was stroking her daughter's hair and kissing her cheeks. I wondered if Scarlett would ever be brave enough to tell her mum how she felt when her mum spoke to her in a mean way. I hoped she would.

After we'd used the bathroom and had something to eat and drink, we sat with a police officer and told him all about what had happened. As soon as we mentioned that we'd found at skeleton, he paused the interview to make some phone calls. I guessed he couldn't just take our word for it that the remains were of an old pirate and hundreds of years old.

"You can't just walk into the mountain," said Josh. "It's deadly in there."

"Yes, there are traps everywhere!" said Scarlett.

"Be on your guard at all times," I said.

We explained about the booby traps and he went a bit pale, before saying they'd organize a team of experts to go inside and make it all safe. He took lots of notes and said that they'd need to speak to us again, but for now we could go home. Even though we could have travelled home with our families, Scarlett, Josh and I agreed that we wanted to travel back together.

We climbed into the school minibus and slumped on to the same seats that we'd travelled up in. This time there were no awkward silences, and the bus was filled with chatting and laughter as we recounted everything that had happened.

Mr Hearn and Ms Bell listened to us all the way. Occasionally they asked us a question like, "Where did you learn how to tie a sling so well, Scarlett?" and, "How deep was the hole you fell into, Vincent?" But mostly they just listened with smiles on their faces.

For the last part of the drive we fell into a relaxed quietness and I put my head against the window and watched the roads become more recognizable.

We passed the industrial estate with the big Let's Go Camp! shop where I'd gone with Mum to get the last few bits for the trip. That seemed like a lifetime ago. So much had changed.

I was nearly home.

I was exhausted, covered in dirt and very smelly, but I was travelling with my friends and I felt very, very happy.

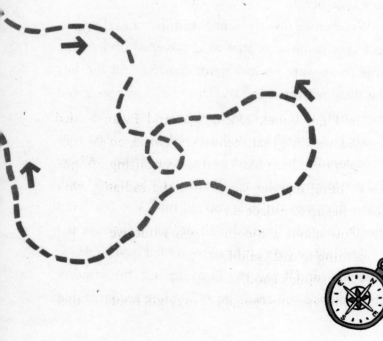

Chapter Thirty-Six

Back with my Feet Firmly on the Ground

When I got home, Mum, Dad and Ewan busied around me while I sat, feeling a bit dazed, on the sofa. I was so tired I felt like I could sleep sitting upright. Ewan hung my wet jacket over the radiator while Mum began to unlace my boots.

"How about a nice hot bath while we get you something to eat?" said Dad.

"That sounds good," I said.

Mum eased my foot out of my right boot and then

my left, and then she started to unpeel my saturated socks.

"These boots weren't so waterproof after all," she said. "We'll have to get some… Oh, Vincent! Your foot! That looks so painful."

The red-raw blister on the back of my heel looked worse than ever. There hadn't been time to rebandage it.

"That's *so* odd," said Dad. He looked closely at my heel and then picked up the boot and inspected it. "These were really comfortable for Ewan."

I swallowed and bit on my lip for a moment. And then I took a deep breath.

"That's the thing, though, Dad. They are Ewan's boots and they fit Ewan's feet. They weren't comfortable for me but you wouldn't listen," I said. "And … and you can't mould me to be like him, just like you can't mould his boots to fit my feet. I'm … I'm my own person."

Dad blinked at me.

"Oh, Vincent. Is that what you think we've been doing?" he said. "You think we've been trying to change you to be more like Ewan?"

I nodded.

"I like doing different things, Dad. I don't want to

go climbing mountains or play tennis. I just want you to see me for who I am. I'm not a copy of anyone else."

I glanced up at Ewan, who looked very uncomfortable. I didn't want him to feel bad.

"I'm proud of everything you've achieved, Ewan," I carried on. "I really miss you not living here. But … but sometimes it's hard to be your brother, you know?" Ewan nodded and gave me a small smile. "I don't want you to stop being brilliant. I just want you, Dad, and you, Mum, to see me as Vincent."

Mum came forward and kissed me on the cheek.

"I'm so sorry, darling," she said. "We didn't mean to make you feel bad. We just wanted you to be happy and to not miss out on things. I guess we shouldn't have pressured you to go on the weekend."

"It's OK, Mum," I said.

I looked up at Dad, and he crouched down and put his hand on my knee.

"I am more proud of you, Vincent, than you can possibly imagine," he said. "And I'm so sorry that I haven't been very good at showing you. I'll try to do better from now on."

He threw his arms around me and this time I let him give me a really big hug.

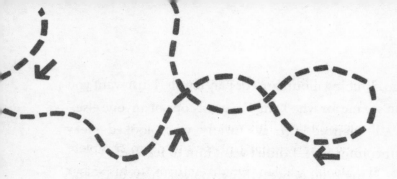

Chapter Thirty-Seven

Battle Doom Finale

The Saturday after the Wilderness Warriors Weekend I finally got a chance to do some gaming. Since being home I'd been busy with school and spending time with Mum, Dad and Ewan in the evenings. Ewan and I had even been to the playing fields to kick a ball about. I wasn't that good but we still had a laugh, and I was surprised how much I'd actually enjoyed it.

I switched on the console and sat in Ewan's squeaky seat, waiting for the game to load. The usual message appeared on the screen.

Hello, butterfingers55

My fingers tingled. This was it.

I knew exactly what I needed to do to complete *Battle Doom*. Fabian would return to his town triumphant and a hero.

I picked up my controller and started the game. I watched Fabian's back moving with his breaths as he stood beside the old well where I'd left him. All I needed to do was wait for the travelling salesman to appear.

I walked around in the dirt for a while. The place was deserted, and there were no other characters around to interact with. Next I checked my inventory and looked at the Scorpion Sword with its empty hole, waiting for the missing diamond.

I went back to the game and circled around the well a few times, and then, from behind a gnarly-looking tree, the hawker appeared. He was dressed exactly the same, wearing a brown hooded cape, dirty trousers and boots. He approached me, looking left and right as he did. No wonder I'd thought that he was being shifty.

"Buy my wares, young man? Buy my wares?" he said, still checking around him.

I stood and waited to see if he was going to do the same thing he always did.

His narrow eyes looked back at me. Then his hand reached into his pocket, and he took out the dirty yellowy stone. It wasn't as big as Walter Morgan's and not nearly as impressive, but I could see exactly what it was now.

"Remember, beauty can be found within the underestimated," he said.

I took a step towards him, and then I went into my inventory, chose my purse and selected a few coins. I gave them to the hawker and he took them, shook his head and held out a grubby-looking hand for more.

I ended up giving him all of my coins, but I knew it was worth it. After this I wouldn't need them any more.

The hawker took my remaining coins and checked around us once again before slowly handing over the diamond. As I held it in my hand he hurried away and ducked back behind a tree.

This was it.

I had the final piece to complete the game.

I looked at the yellow stone for a few more seconds, then clicked into my inventory and the Scorpion Sword. I slotted the diamond into the missing hole and waited.

The game paused for a few seconds and then it returned to a signpost which said: *Welcome To Riverlock*. It was Fabian's hometown. And Fabian was standing beside the sign with the Scorpion Sword in his hand.

I walked him along the path, on to the street, excited to see how his family and friends were going to react when they saw the incredible thing that he had achieved. I couldn't wait to find out the true meaning behind the Scorpion Sword and why it was so important to everyone in the town.

But as Fabian walked past the first house, a graphic spun towards me and centred in the middle of the screen:

MISSION COMPLETED

And then the screen faded to black.

I couldn't believe it.

"WHAT?" I shouted. "Is that IT?"

What about the hero's welcome? Fabian had been through so much and I wanted everyone to see how strong he had been and how he had overcome all of his problems and proved them all wrong. But then I guessed it was all about the taking part in the first place. I reached to switch off the screen when a tiny light flickered in the corner. It was a glass storm lantern, like the one we'd used in Fortune Mountain, slowing coming into focus. The glow from the candle lit the space around it – a dark and dank-looking cave. It reminded me of what we'd seen, and I could almost smell the damp air and hear those weird moaning noises again. Just then, Fabian stepped out from the shadows and walked towards me, his eyes still pained and desperate, even though he'd completed his quest. He bent down and picked up the lantern and it swung back and forth from his fingers. Then he turned and walked into a dark, narrow tunnel, the light from the lantern fading to nothing. The screen was black again and some words materialized on the screen.

COMING SOON ...

BATTLE DOOM 2 – THE MOUNTAIN LABYRINTH

There was another *Battle Doom*?! My heart leaped! That was amazing!

The doorbell rang and Mum shouted up the stairs.

"Vincent! Your friends are here."

I switched off the console, jumped out of Ewan's chair and grabbed my jacket, then thumped downstairs. Scarlett, Josh and Lena were standing on the doorstep. Lena had her arm in a cast and sling, but she had a big smile on her face.

"All right?" I said. "How's your arm?"

"It's not so painful now," she said. "I'll be back at school on Monday."

"Great!" I said.

School had transformed for me since our weekend together and I was even beginning to enjoy it. I spent a lot of time hanging around with Josh, and Scarlett also joined us now and then. She'd fallen out with Melanie and Holly again and said she wasn't going to bother being friends with them any more. In fact, it was Scarlett's idea that we got together to go to a new bowling alley that had opened a few weeks ago.

Mum hovered around with a soppy smile on her face. I knew this was my cue to exit the house before she said something embarrassing.

"You all have a wonderful time, won't you?" she said. "No going off on any secret missions now, Lena. OK?"

Lena flushed a little. "I promise," she said.

Mum closed the door behind us and we headed down the street. We were silent for a few seconds, adjusting to being together in completely different circumstances.

"I'll bowl for you if you like, Lena?" said Scarlett. "Although you probably won't get any points I'm afraid."

Lena laughed. "That'll be great. Thanks," she said.

We walked along in silence for a while.

I cleared my throat. "Everything feels a bit different now, doesn't it?" I said.

"Yeah," said Josh. "I know what you mean. There's no rain for a start!"

"What happened with the diamond?" said Scarlett.

"The British Museum has it," said Lena. "They are going to look into its history and it'll be declared as treasure. I guess at some point people will be able to go and see it on display."

I noticed that Lena was carrying a rucksack over her shoulder. Not one like she had for camping, but big enough all the same.

"Are you going somewhere, Lena?" I asked. She looked at me and I gestured to the bag.

"Oh, no. These are just some files I found in amongst Grandpa's stuff," she said. "I thought I'd have a read through while you're all bowling."

Scarlett looked at me and Josh, and then she stopped.

"Lena?" she said. "You're not thinking of going on another mission, are you?"

Josh and I stood beside Scarlett as Lena carried on a few paces. Then she turned and faced us. Her eyes were bright and shiny, and even though I hadn't known her that well for very long, I knew that look meant she was excited about something.

"I was going to wait until we were at the bowling alley before I said anything."

"Go on," said Josh.

Lena bit her lip and a huge grin spread across her face.

"What are your feelings on the Loch Ness Monster?" she said.

Read more bestselling, award-winning novels by

LISA THOMPSON

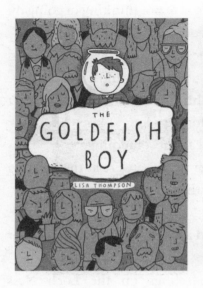

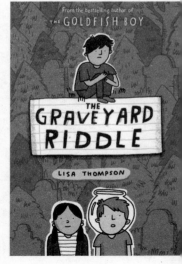